Stitch
-by-
Stitch

JANE BULL

LONDON, NEW YORK, MUNICH,
MELBOURNE, and DELHI

DESIGN AND TEXT Jane Bull
PHOTOGRAPHER Andy Crawford
SENIOR EDITOR Carrie Love
EDITORS Alexander Cox, Lee Wilson
US EDITOR Margaret Parrish
DESIGNER Lauren Rosier

PRODUCTION EDITOR Siu Chan
PRODUCTION CONTROLLER Claire Pearson

CREATIVE DIRECTOR Jane Bull
CATAGORY PUBLISHER Mary Ling

First American Edition, 2012
Published in the United States by
DK Publishing
375 Hudson Street,
New York, New York 10014

12 13 14 15 16 10 9 8 7 6 5 4 3 2 1
001—181751—04/12

Published in Great Britain by Dorling Kindersley Limited.

A catalog record for this book
is available from the Library of Congress.

ISBN: 978-0-7566-9022-9
DK books are available at special discounts when purchased in bulk
for sales promotions, premiums, fund-raising, or educational use.
For details, contact: DK Publishing Special Markets,
375 Hudson Street, New York, New York 10014 or
SpecialSales@dk.com.

Color reproduction by
Media Development Printing Ltd. UK
Printed and bound in China
by Hung Hing

Discover more at
www.dk.com

This book's for my
needlecraft teacher,
Barbara Owen
(who's also my mom).

Crochet

Stitch-by-Stitch

is all about needlecraft
introducing beginners to embroidery,
crochet, patchwork, appliqué, knitting,
and needlepoint. It teaches the basic
techniques and then takes them a step
further, showing how to use the new
skills to create fun and beautiful projects,
revitalizing the skills our grandmothers
took for granted and bringing them
up to date.

Embroidery

Patchwork

Knitting

Needlepoint

Appliqué

Contents

Store your essential sewing materials in little boxes.

SOFT-TOY FILLING is used for stuffing projects such as patchwork balls, pillows, and knitted dolls. It is a lightweight material that produces an even stuffing.

FELT is available in lots of colors. It's easy to cut into small shapes and is useful as a backing material.

Felt is perfect for projects because the edges don't fray.

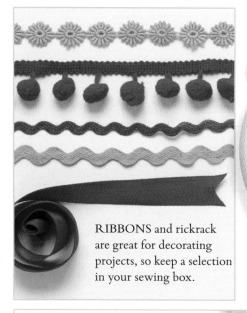

RIBBONS and rickrack are great for decorating projects, so keep a selection in your sewing box.

Keep on hand

Here is a selection of equipment and materials that will come in handy when making the projects in this book.

Self-covering buttons can be found in craft stores.

Safety pins for making brooches

Brightly colored buttons

PINKING SHEARS are special scissors with zigzag-shaped blades that create a zigzag edge in the fabric when it's cut. The zigzag prevents the material from fraying.

COTTON FABRIC is lightweight and can be used for embroidery projects, appliqué, and patchwork.

A button box

Sewing basics

All the projects covered in this book will require a handy kit like this, in addition to the materials and equipment needed for each technique. You will also want to master some basic sewing skills to complete the projects included.

Sewing box

You could buy a sewing box and use it to store all your sewing equipment and materials, but why not make one out of a shoebox instead?

Handy tip

Remember to keep this kit with you when making the projects in this book.

Sewing thread

Needle threader

Embroidery scissors

Needle case

Dressmakers' scissors

Pin cushion

Thimble

Tape measure

Thread

It's handy to have a selection of different-colored sewing threads on hand so you can match them to your fabrics. Needle threaders are useful, too.

Needles,

Sewing needles are usually thin, with either a small eye or a long, thin eye. Keep a selection of needles in a needle case.

Pins

You'll need pins in a lot of the sewing projects. A pin cushion keeps your pins neatly stored and always on hand. Glass-headed pins are pretty and easy to see if dropped.

Scissors

It helps to own several good, sharp scissors, each suited to a particular job. Embroidery scissors are best for snipping threads; dressmakers' scissors are ideal for cutting large pieces of fabric.

Thimble

You wear a thimble on the middle finger of your hand that holds the needle. It is used to push the needle through the fabric and keeps your finger from getting sore.

Tape measure

Some projects will have thread, fabric, and yarn that needs to be measured exactly.

Threading a needle

Threading a needle can be difficult. A needle with a larger eye will make it easier, or you can use a needle threader. Use sharp scissors to cut the thread.

Thread length?
If you work with thread that is too long it will get tangled, slowing you down. Cut a length of thread about the length of your lower arm, from the end of your fingers to your elbow.

Thread the needle.

Double the thread and knot the end.

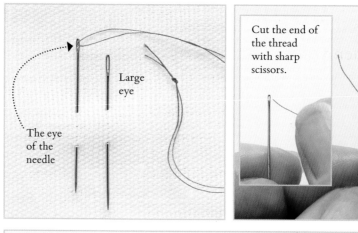

The eye of the needle

Large eye

Cut the end of the thread with sharp scissors.

Push the thread through the eye of the needle.

USING A NEEDLE THREADER

1. Push the threader wire through the eye of the needle.

2. Put the end of the thread though the wire.

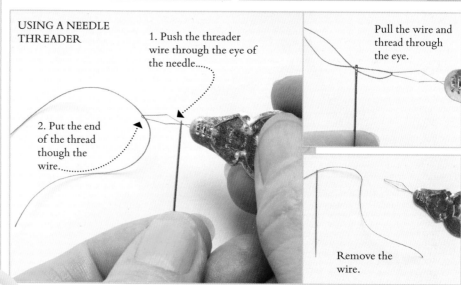

Pull the wire and thread through the eye.

Remove the wire.

Sewing on a button

1

First, secure the thread in the fabric. Then put the button onto the needle and drop it down the thread.

2

Push the needle back through the holes in the button.

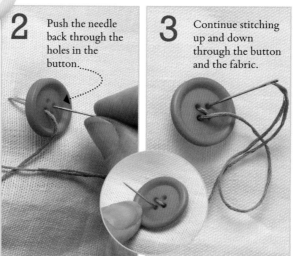

3

Continue stitching up and down through the button and the fabric.

4

To secure the button, bring the thread up under the button.

Sew backward and forward behind the button, then cut the thread.

Sewing stitches

Here are the stitches that are used for the projects. They all have a different job to do when you are joining fabric together for pillows, bags, and patchwork pieces.

How to start and finish

Make a knot at the end of the thread, and begin stitching. To end a row of stitches, make a very small stitch but do not pull it tight. Bring the thread back up through the loop and pull tight. Do this once more in the same spot, then cut the thread.

Running stitch

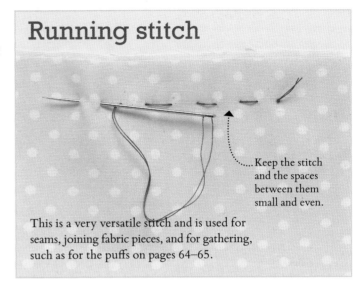

Keep the stitch and the spaces between them small and even.

This is a very versatile stitch and is used for seams, joining fabric pieces, and for gathering, such as for the puffs on pages 64–65.

Backstitch

Make the stitch, then bring the needle back to the spot where the last stitch was finished.

This is the strongest stitch. It makes a continuous line of stitches so it is best used when two pieces of fabric, like the sides of a bag, need to be sewed securely.

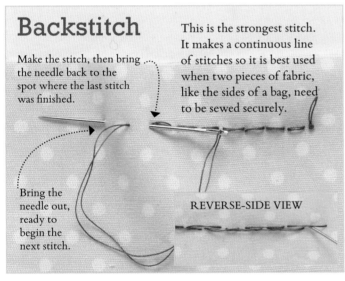

Bring the needle out, ready to begin the next stitch.

REVERSE-SIDE VIEW

Basting stitch

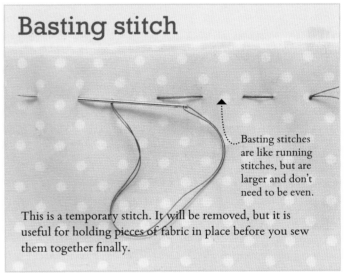

Basting stitches are like running stitches, but are larger and don't need to be even.

This is a temporary stitch. It will be removed, but it is useful for holding pieces of fabric in place before you sew them together finally.

Overstitch

Insert the needle diagonally from the back of the fabric.

Pick up only two or three threads of fabric.

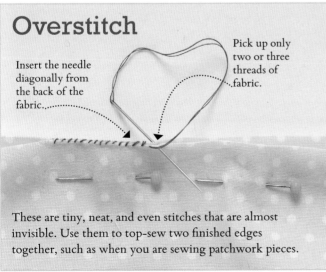

These are tiny, neat, and even stitches that are almost invisible. Use them to top-sew two finished edges together, such as when you are sewing patchwork pieces.

Slip stitch

Use a slip stitch when you want the stitches to be invisible. This stitch is made by slipping the thread under a fold of fabric. It is often used to join two folded edges, such as the openings of pillows.

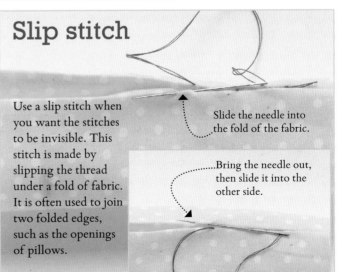

Slide the needle into the fold of the fabric.

Bring the needle out, then slide it into the other side.

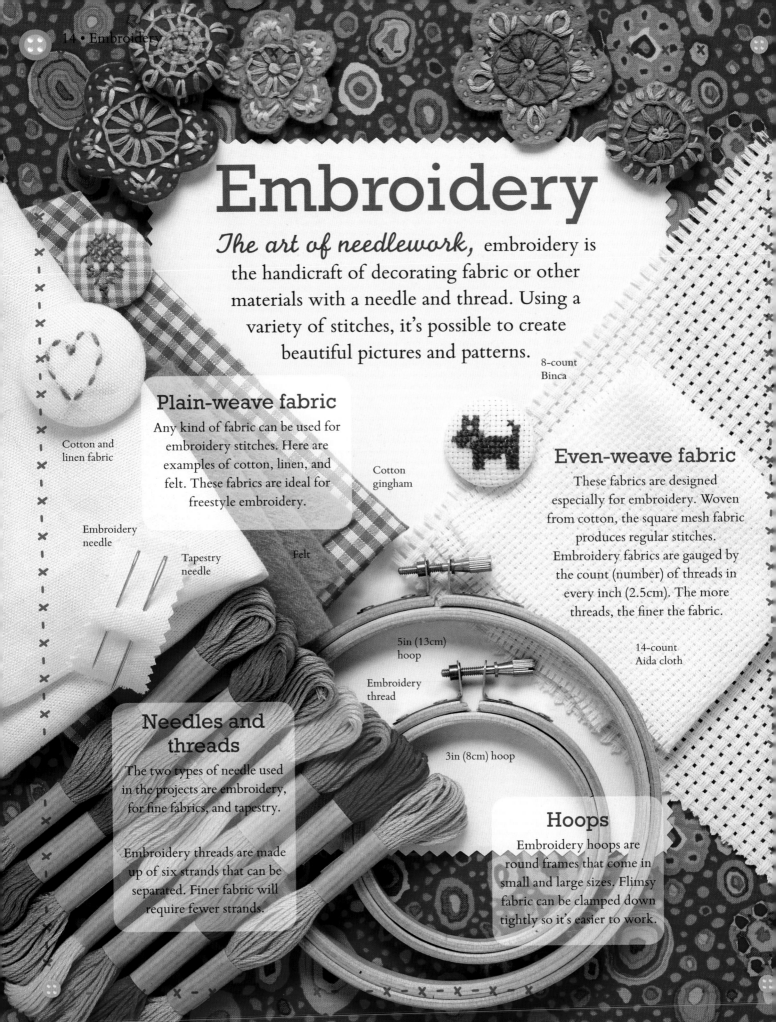

Embroidery

The art of needlework, embroidery is the handicraft of decorating fabric or other materials with a needle and thread. Using a variety of stitches, it's possible to create beautiful pictures and patterns.

Plain-weave fabric

Any kind of fabric can be used for embroidery stitches. Here are examples of cotton, linen, and felt. These fabrics are ideal for freestyle embroidery.

Cotton and linen fabric

Embroidery needle

Tapestry needle

Felt

Cotton gingham

8-count Binca

Even-weave fabric

These fabrics are designed especially for embroidery. Woven from cotton, the square mesh fabric produces regular stitches. Embroidery fabrics are gauged by the count (number) of threads in every inch (2.5cm). The more threads, the finer the fabric.

14-count Aida cloth

5in (13cm) hoop

Embroidery thread

3in (8cm) hoop

Needles and threads

The two types of needle used in the projects are embroidery, for fine fabrics, and tapestry.

Embroidery threads are made up of six strands that can be separated. Finer fabric will require fewer strands.

Hoops

Embroidery hoops are round frames that come in small and large sizes. Flimsy fabric can be clamped down tightly so it's easier to work.

Designs on even-weave fabric

This example shows how the different thread counts affect the design. Notice how the same motif, using the same number of stitches, changes size.

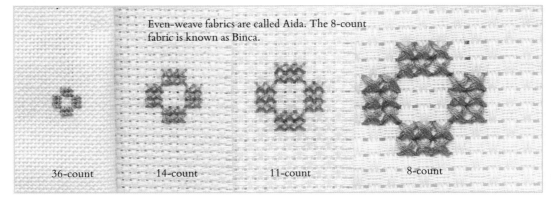

Even-weave fabrics are called Aida. The 8-count fabric is known as Binca.

36-count   14-count   11-count   8-count

Transferring designs

EVEN-WEAVE FABRIC

For this type of fabric, designs are made up of squares, with each square representing a stitch.

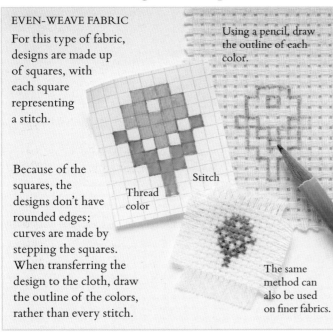

Using a pencil, draw the outline of each color.

Thread color

Stitch

Because of the squares, the designs don't have rounded edges; curves are made by stepping the squares. When transferring the design to the cloth, draw the outline of the colors, rather than every stitch.

The same method can also be used on finer fabrics.

PLAIN-WEAVE FABRIC

Any shape can be achieved using plain-weave fabric, which is ideal for freestyle stitching.

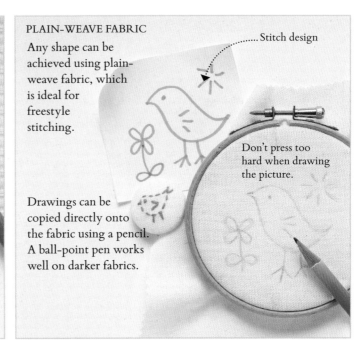

Stitch design

Don't press too hard when drawing the picture.

Drawings can be copied directly onto the fabric using a pencil. A ball-point pen works well on darker fabrics.

How to use a hoop

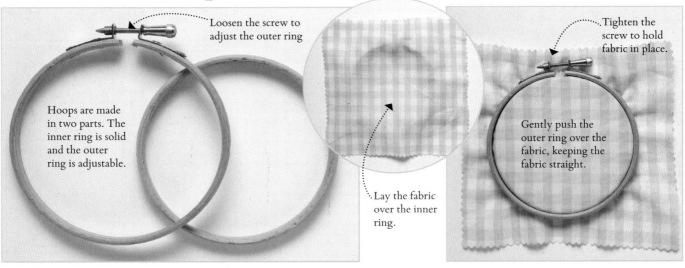

Loosen the screw to adjust the outer ring

Hoops are made in two parts. The inner ring is solid and the outer ring is adjustable.

Lay the fabric over the inner ring.

Tighten the screw to hold fabric in place.

Gently push the outer ring over the fabric, keeping the fabric straight.

Stitches gallery

Running stitch

This stitch forms a dotted line. The stitches can vary in length, depending on the effect you want.

Make stitches by bringing the needle in and out.

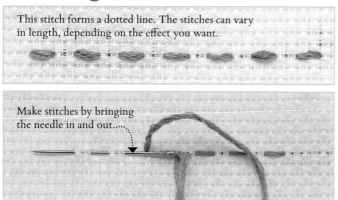

Backstitch

Backstitch creates a continuous line.

Make a stitch, then reinsert the needle where the stitch began.

Pull the needle through.

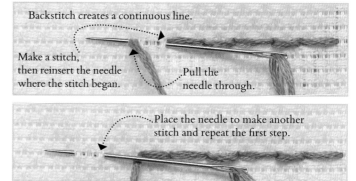

Place the needle to make another stitch and repeat the first step.

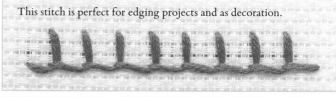

Cross-stitch

Cross-stitches can be worked in rows or singly.

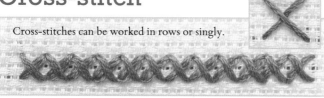

Make diagonal stitches in the same direction.

Bring the needle out here, ready to begin the next stitch.

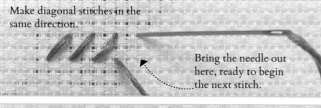

To complete the "X" shapes, work back across the row, using the same hole as the previous stitch.

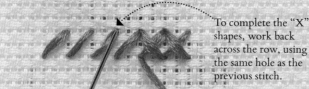

Blanket stitch

This stitch is perfect for edging projects and as decoration.

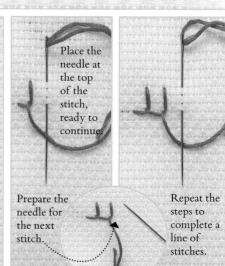

Bring the needle out and back into the fabric. Keep the thread under the needle.

Place the needle at the top of the stitch, ready to continue.

Prepare the needle for the next stitch.

Repeat the steps to complete a line of stitches.

Chain stitch

This decorative stitch looks like a chain.

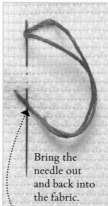

Single chain stitches can look like leaves or petals.

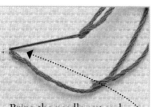

Bring the needle out and then back next to where it came out.

Pull the thread through until it forms a loop.

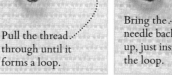

Bring the needle back up, just inside the loop.

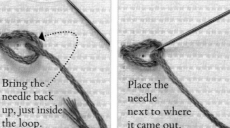

Place the needle next to where it came out.

Make a new loop and repeat the steps to continue making a chain.

Crown stitch

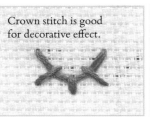

Crown stitch is good for decorative effect.

Bring the thread around to form a loose stitch.

Make a stitch over the stitch to hold it in place.

Continue making stitches.

A third stitch completes the crown stitch.

French knot

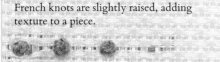

French knots are slightly raised, adding texture to a piece.

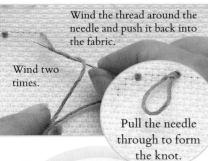

Wind the thread around the needle and push it back into the fabric.

Wind two times.

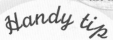

Pull the needle through to form the knot.

Handy tip

Cut a piece of thread that is about the length from your fingertips to your elbow to avoid knots and tangles.

Threading a needle

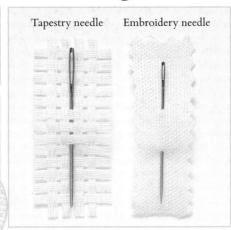

Tapestry needle   Embroidery needle

Separate the six strands.

To separate the six strands, hold three strands with one hand and slide the other hand down the length of the thread.

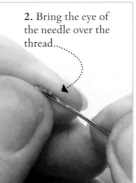

1. To thread three or six strands of thread, loop the thread over the needle and pull tightly.

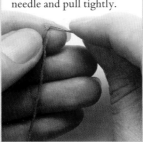

2. Bring the eye of the needle over the thread...

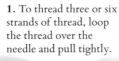

3. Pull the thread through the eye of the needle...

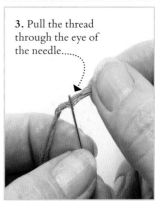

Starting and stopping

STARTING OFF

Knot the thread and bring it up through the fabric.

Hold the hoop in one hand and use the other to sew the design.

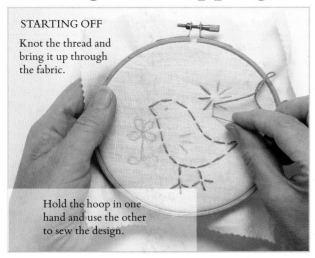

FASTENING OFF

Turn the work over. To secure the thread, pass it under the stitches nearby.

Trim the thread.

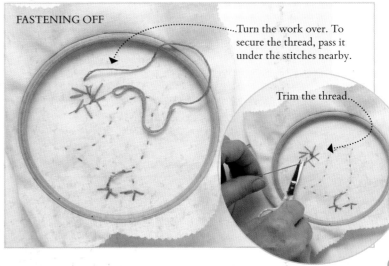

Running stitch

Single chain stitch

Garden bird

Doodles make great buttons. See pages 34–35.

Use a running stitch to follow the outline of your doodle.

Kitty kat

Add color to your doodles by using colored thread.

Use different sizes of embroidery hoop.

Embroidery hoops can be used as picture frames. Just leave your work in place, gather up the fabric on the reverse side, and tape it in place.

Love hearts

Fireworks

Stitching doodles
A great way
to use your doodles is to recreate them in stitches. Even simple scribbles when stitched can be to made into something special.

Happy cloud

...Choose fabric that is lightweight and has a loose weave, such as this cotton fabric shown.

How to stitch a doodle

When you've chosen your doodle, either copy it by drawing it directly onto the fabric with a pencil or transfer it using tracing paper (see page 120).

You will need

• Your doodles
• Embroidery hoop
• Cotton or linen fabric • Embroidery threads • Embroidery needle
• Embroidery needle with pointed end
• Pencil • Sewing needle and thread

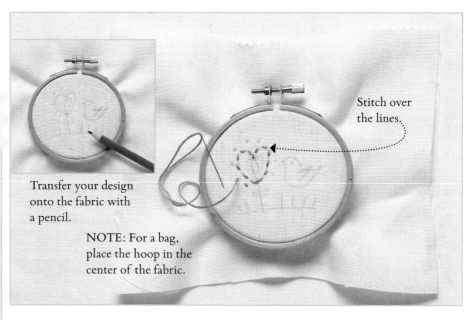

Transfer your design onto the fabric with a pencil.

NOTE: For a bag, place the hoop in the center of the fabric.

Stitch over the lines.

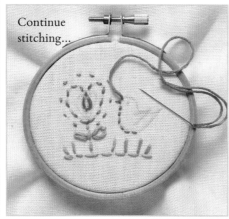

Continue stitching...

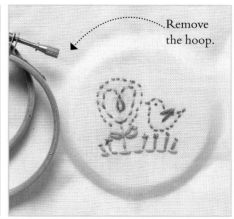

Remove the hoop.

How to make a bag

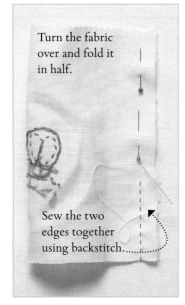

Turn the fabric over and fold it in half.

Sew the two edges together using backstitch.

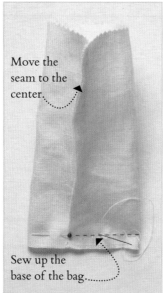

Move the seam to the center.

Sew up the base of the bag.

Turn the bag right side out.

The finished design will appear on the front.

Gift bags

If you are looking for something to wrap a gift in, try putting it into one of these little bags and tie it up with a ribbon... now you have two gifts in one!

For sweet smells, fill with dried lavender.

Using simple stitches like blanket stitch, chain stitch, and straight stitch, you can make really colorful designs.

Felt flowers

To make a bunch of flowers, save all those pretty scraps of felt and transform them into bright and cheery blooms. Play with the colors of the felt and thread for dazzling effects.

Attach pins to the backs of the flowers to make charming brooches.

You will need

- Colorful felt scraps
- Embroidery thread
- Embroidery needle

Small lengths of embroidery thread.

Save small pieces of felt for projects like this.

Flower templates

Place tracing paper over these shapes and trace over them with pencil. Transfer the design onto thin cardboard. Cut out the cardboard and use the shapes for the felt flower.

See page 120 for transferring designs.

How to stitch a flower

To make a flower shape, lay the template on a piece of felt. Carefully draw around the edge of the cardboard and around the center circle. This will show you where to start the center of the flower.

Felt.

Cardboard template.

You will need

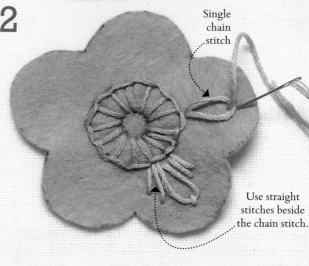

Felt shape for backing.

Embroidery needle

Felt shape for flower front.

Embroidery thread in different colors.

1 Start stitching the center of the flower.

Blanket stitch

2 Single chain stitch

Use straight stitches beside the chain stitch.

3 Sew the front and back pieces together.

Running stitch

4 Safety pin

Sew over the attached side of the pin, as shown here.

Your flower embroidery can be used to cover buttons, too. See how on pages 34–35.

Brighten up your T-shirts, jackets, and jeans with colorful stitches.

Sewing flowers on your clothes

Use the flower template to draw out the area you want to sew. Then simply follow the steps for the felt flowers.

Choose where you want the stitching to go and mark it out as with the felt.

Flower patch

Use the flowers as patches—sew them on to clothes and bags.

Pin a flower to the garment.

Sew the flower in position using a running stitch.

Decorated beany hat

You will need

Patterned cotton fabric

Buttons and ribbons

Embroidery thread

YOU WILL ALSO NEED
• Embroidery hoop, large enough to fit your template • Embroidery needle • Soft-toy stuffing

Pretty birdies

Collect pieces of patterned fabric to create these cute little birds. Use embroidery stitches to give the birds features and have fun with the fabric print, following the flower shapes to create a detailed, special effect.

How to make a bird

Place the fabric in the hoop.

Draw around the cardboard shape with a pencil (see template on p121).

Decorate the bird shape with a variety of stitches and colors.

Create bird features such as wings, an eye, and a tail.

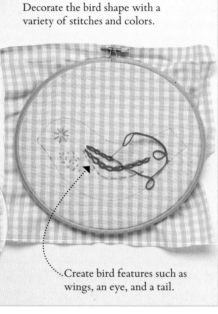

Remove the hoop.

Cut around the bird shape.

...Cut out another bird shape for the back.

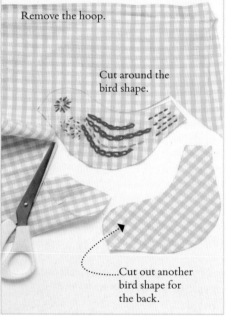

Pin the two bird shapes together...

Fill the bird with stuffing.

Sew the pieces together using the blanket stitch.

Leave an opening for the stuffing.

Continue stitching to close the opening.

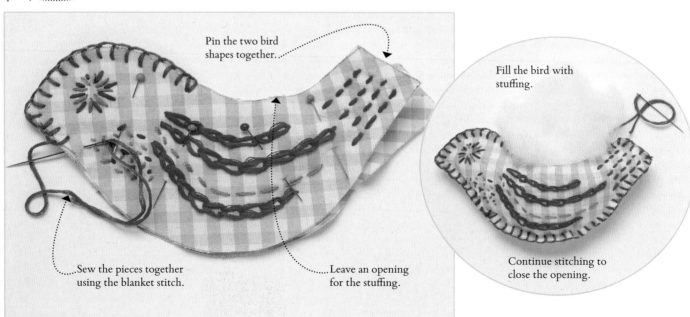

Handy tip

Why not use the design on the patterned fabric to guide your stitches? Follow the outline of the petals and add chain-stitch leaves using threads in contrasting colors. Finish by sewing on button eyes.

Hanging pretty

To make hanging birds, cut a length of ribbon 8in (20cm) long. Fold it in half and sew it to the bird, adding a button for extra decoration.

Gingham cross-stitch

Gingham is a type of cotton fabric that is available in an array of colors. Its checkered design comes in different sizes, from tiny checks to huge squares. Make the most of this ready-made pattern to try out your cross-stitch.

You will need

• Gingham fabric • Fabric for back • Embroidery hoop • Embroidery needle and thread • Soft-toy filling • Sewing needle and thread

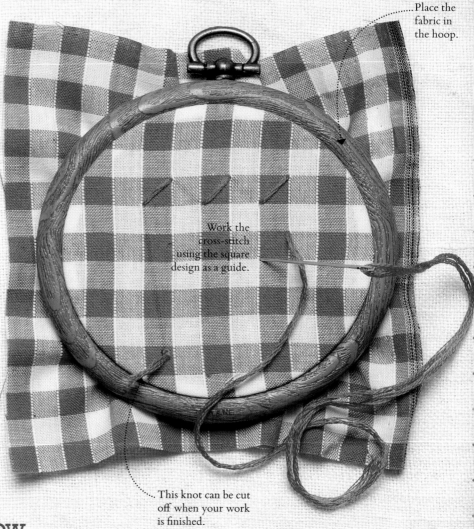

Place the fabric in the hoop.

Work the cross-stitch using the square design as a guide.

This knot can be cut off when your work is finished.

How to make a pillow

1

Put the fabric pieces together, right sides facing

Pin the two pieces of fabric together.

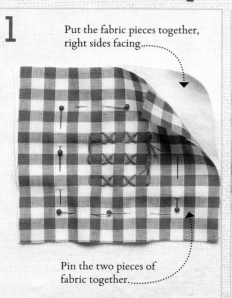

2

Sew the fabric pieces together.

Leave a space at the top for filling.

Cut out the fabric ⅓in (7mm) away from the stitching.

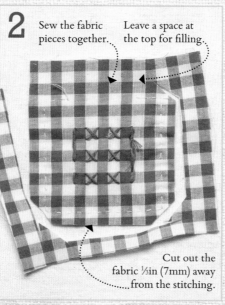

3

Turn the pillow case right sides out.

Fill the pillow case, making sure not to overfill it.

Using a sewing needle and thread, carefully sew together the opening.

Simple sampler

Try out your skills with a sampler. Traditionally, samplers were used to practice embroidery skills. Here is an easy design of hearts and flowers to get you started.

Frame your finished work.

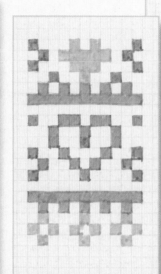

Each square represents a stitch and shows which color of thread to use.

You will need

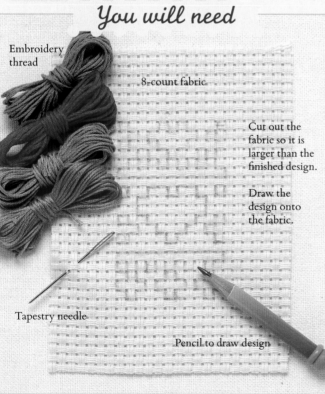

Embroidery thread

8-count fabric

Cut out the fabric so it is larger than the finished design.

Draw the design onto the fabric.

Tapestry needle

Pencil to draw design

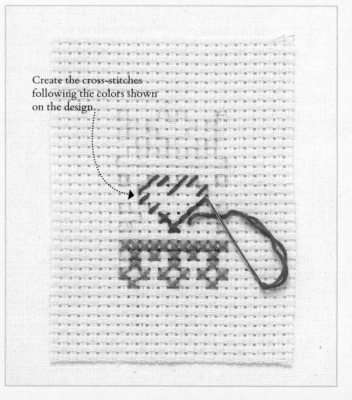

Create the cross-stitches following the colors shown on the design.

Good gifts

These homemade samplers make perfect gifts. Frame and attach some ribbon so they can be hung.

Make it larger

Use the alternative template to create a larger sampler. Remember, it's not necessary to draw the entire design onto the fabric; the first few rows can act as a guide.

See pages 122–123 for templates.

Pictures in stitches

Big and small You can make the same picture in a different size by using a fabric of a different thread count.

You will need

• 8-count and 14-count cross-stitch fabric • Embroidery needle and thread

Make a picture

Embroidery needle with rounded end

8-count fabric

14-count fabric

Embroidery needle with pointed end

Embroidery thread

1

Each square on the template represents one stitch.

2

Use a pencil, but don't press too hard.

Copy the picture onto the fabric.

For a smaller picture, work in the same way but use a 14-count fabric.

Use three strands of thread to sew through the smaller holes.

3 Work the cross-stitch from the bottom up.

Keep the stitches facing in the same direction.

4

For a decorative edge, allow the fabric to fray.

Cut the fabric to the required size, then pull the strands of fabric away.

See pages 34–35 to learn how to make buttons.

Glue your picture to the front of greeting cards.

Design your own key chain.

There are lots of ways to use the pictures you create. From greeting cards to buttons, and box lids to key chains, all make perfect gifts.

Customize your stuff by attaching different-sized pictures to your belongings. Make a matching set in no time!

Beautiful buttons

Like precious gems covering these button bases with your work can make even the tiniest piece of embroidery look special. What a perfect way to use up scrap fabric and short ends of thread. Sew onto your clothes to replace your buttons or wear as a brooch.

You will need

Scraps of fabric

Leftover embroidery threads

Sewing thread

Sewing needle

Button template for fabric size

Button base top and bottom

Embroidery needle

How to make a button

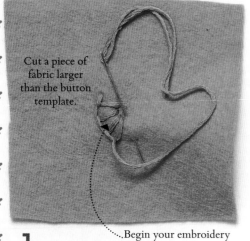

Cut a piece of fabric larger than the button template.

1 ....Begin your embroidery in the center.

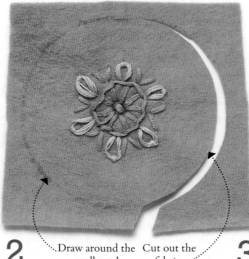

2 ....Draw around the cardboard template. Cut out the fabric....

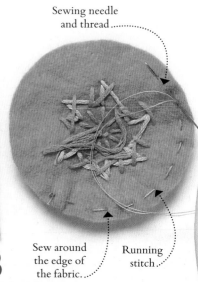

Sewing needle and thread

3 Sew around the edge of the fabric.... Running stitch....

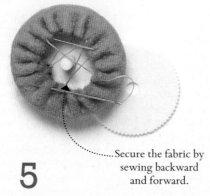

Place the button top in the center of the fabric....

4 ....Gently pull the thread to gather the fabric.

5 ....Secure the fabric by sewing backward and forward.

6 ....Press the back of the button down firmly.

Felt flower design
(see pages 22–24).

Stitch over the designs on
printed fabric (see page 27).

Cross-stitch motifs
(see pages 32–33).

Buttons galore:

Experiment with the embroidery you have tried with the
other projects on the previous pages. These small areas are
great for practicing your skills.

Needlepoint

Also known as tapestry, or canvas work, needlepoint is the craft of stitching onto a firm, open-weave canvas. The stitches are worked on a canvas grid and tightly stitched so that none of the background shows through.

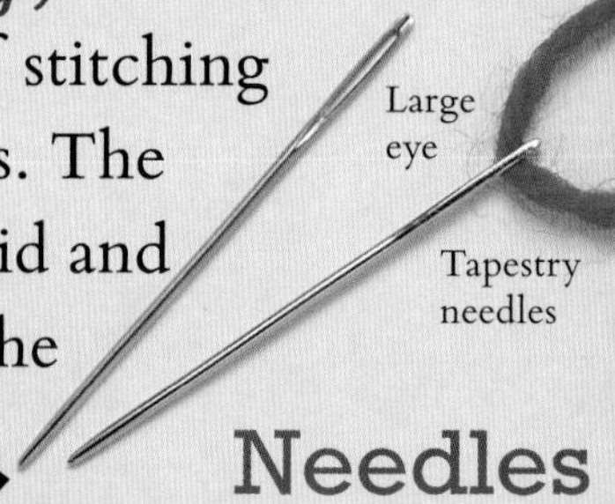

Large eye

Tapestry needles

Rounded end

Needles

Needlepoint, or tapestry, needles have rounded ends. This helps to keep the point from catching on the canvas threads. The large eye makes it easy to thread.

Canvas

Canvas is made of cotton thread that has been treated to make it very stiff. It is sized by mesh sizes, or thread count per inch (2.5cm); for example, "10 count" means that there are 10 threads to an inch (2.5 cm). The sizes range from 5 count to 24 count; the smaller the mesh, the finer the stitches will be. Canvas is sold in craft stores. It comes with preprinted designs as part of a kit or can be bought plain by the yard.

The projects in this book use 10-count canvas— 10 threads per 1in (2.5 cm)

Skeins of tapestry yarn

projects

There are all kinds of needlepoint equipment and materials available, from plastic canvas to kits with printed designs. The items shown here are all you need to complete the projects that follow and to create your own designs, too.

Threads

Needlepoint thread and yarn comes in wool, cotton, or silk. Wool gives the best results on 10-count canvas, since the stitches lay close together, completely hiding the canvas underneath. You can buy it in measured lengths called skeins.

Cutting the canvas

Taping the edges is optional.

Before you start, cut out a piece of canvas. Count the number of stitches required for your design and then decide how much room to leave around the edge, since the canvas needs to be larger than your design. This border can be cut away later or kept, if you want to frame your work.

The image area.

If the yarn keeps catching on the edge of the canvas, use masking tape to cover the edges.

Masking tape

Transferring designs

(See the project pages for designs as well as the templates on pages 120–123.)

Needlepoint designs are made up of squares, with each square representing a stitch. Notice that the stitch doesn't go in the holes of the canvas, but across the threads. The design is just a guide. Create your own design or use one of the templates in this book.

Design your own image on graph paper.

Graph paper

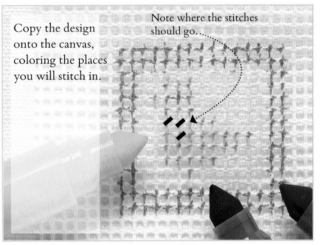

Copy the design onto the canvas, coloring the places you will stitch in.

Note where the stitches should go.

Threading a needle

Cut a piece of yarn 20in (50cm) long, thread the needle, and knot the end of the yarn.

Fold the end of the yarn over the needle and pull it tight.

Pinch the loop between your fingers.

Put the eye of the needle over the loop.

Slide the eye of the needle down the loop.

Pull the yarn through until the short end is out of the eye.

Begin stitching

This design has been made using tent stitch.

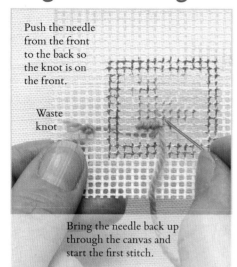

Push the needle from the front to the back so the knot is on the front.

Waste knot

Bring the needle back up through the canvas and start the first stitch.

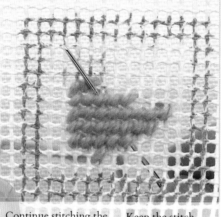

Continue stitching the same color forward and backward.

Keep the stitch facing in the same direction.

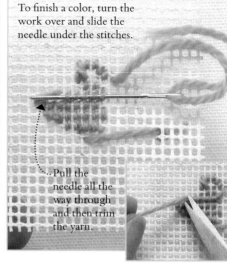

To finish a color, turn the work over and slide the needle under the stitches.

Pull the needle all the way through and then trim the yarn.

Add a new color

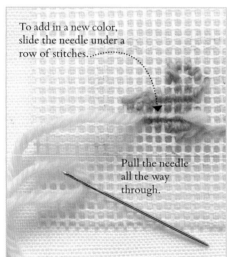

To add in a new color, slide the needle under a row of stitches.

Pull the needle all the way through.

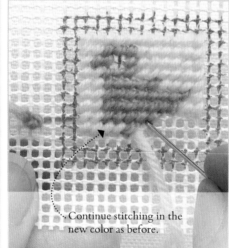

Continue stitching in the new color as before.

Finish the color, turn the work over, and slide the needle under the stitches.

Continue as before.

Finishing off

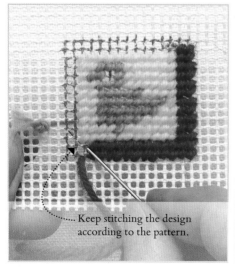

Keep stitching the design according to the pattern.

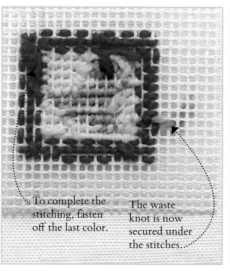

To complete the stitching, fasten off the last color.

The waste knot is now secured under the stitches.

The waste knot can be cut off.

Needlepoint stitches

Simple stitches Although there are lots of different styles of needlepoint stitch to choose from, here are four types of stitch to try in the projects that follow. The simplest is tent stitch, which is a small diagonal stitch. These examples of needlepoint show that by varying the size of the stitch, the direction it goes, and the color combinations, many patterns and designs can be achieved.

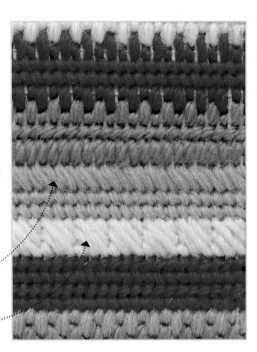

Interlocking straight stitch

Tent stitch

Diagonal stitch

Cushion stitch

DIAGONAL STITCH

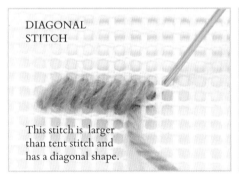

This stitch is larger than tent stitch and has a diagonal shape.

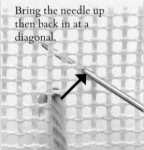

Bring the needle up then back in at a diagonal.

Bring the needle back through the canvas to the front, next to the first stitch.

Repeat steps through the end of the row.

DIAGONAL SQUARE

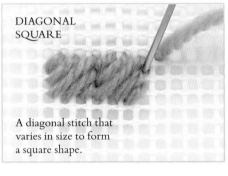

A diagonal stitch that varies in size to form a square shape.

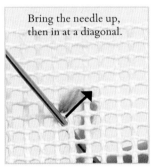

Bring the needle up, then in at a diagonal.

Pull the wool through to the back, then bring back to the front through the hole beneath the second stitch.

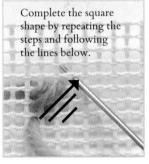

Complete the square shape by repeating the steps and following the lines below.

INTERLOCKING STRAIGHT STITCH

Different heights of straight stitch give an interlocking effect.

Bring the needle out of the canvas...

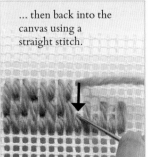

... then back into the canvas using a straight stitch.

Repeat these steps, alternating long and short straight stitches.

Striped pouch

Here's a chance to try out a variety of stitches and play with colors. Create simple striped designs to decorate these handy little pouches—they're great for storing music players.

You will need
- 10-count canvas
- Tapestry yarn in various colors • Tapestry needle
- Felt fabric • Sewing needle and thread

1 Cut the canvas larger than the finished pouch size.

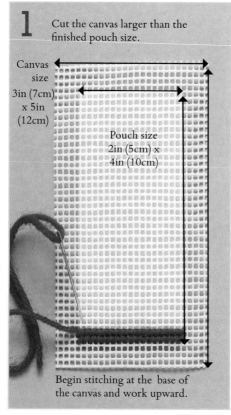

Canvas size 3in (7cm) x 5in (12cm)

Pouch size 2in (5cm) x 4in (10cm)

Begin stitching at the base of the canvas and work upward.

2 Use a pencil to mark the area to be stitched.

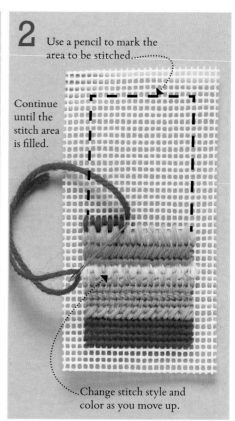

Continue until the stitch area is filled.

Change stitch style and color as you move up.

3 Carefully cut around the canvas.

Don't cut too close or the canvas will come apart.

4 Stitch over the edge of the canvas.

Sew all the way around the edge.

5 Cut the felt the same size as the canvas work.

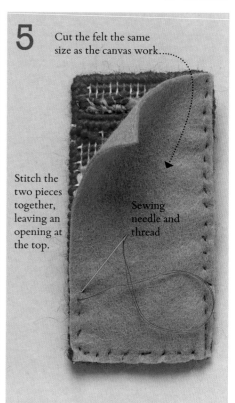

Stitch the two pieces together, leaving an opening at the top.

Sewing needle and thread

Gadget pouch

Perfect for keeping your phone or music player safely tucked away—you can use it for glasses, too.

3in (7cm) x 5in (12cm)

Measure up

Decide what the pouch will be used for—your music player, for example. Measure its height and width, and don't forget how thick the device is, too. Add this to the width, otherwise the pouch will be too tight.

Sewing pouch

Perfect for sewing essentials, such as small, sharp embroidery scissors.

2in (5cm) x 4in (10cm)

3in (7cm) x 5in (12cm)

All squared

See how many patterns you can make simply by using squares. Try the designs shown here, or create your own designs. Make sure to draw them on paper first. These little pillows make pretty pin cushions, but you can make your pillows any size you like.

You will need

Canvas

Tapestry needle

Felt for backing

Stuffing for the pillow

Tapestry yarn

Sewing needle

Cotton thread

How to make a pillow

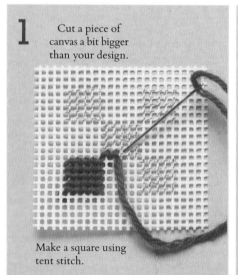

1 Cut a piece of canvas a bit bigger than your design.

Make a square using tent stitch.

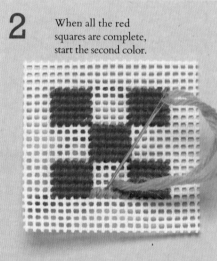

2 When all the red squares are complete, start the second color.

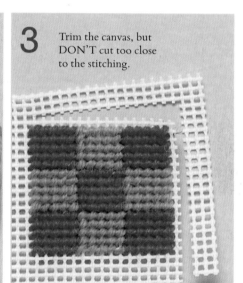

3 Trim the canvas, but DON'T cut too close to the stitching.

4 Sew over the edge of the canvas.

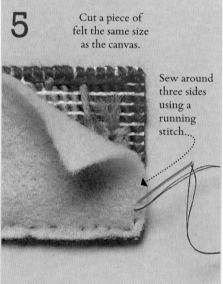

5 Cut a piece of felt the same size as the canvas.

Sew around three sides using a running stitch.

6 Fill the pillow.

Neatly sew up the opening.

The biggest pillow here is 4½in (11cm) x 4½in (11cm). The smallest one is 1½in (4cm) x 1½in (4cm).

Pin cushions

Pixel patches

Just like digital pictures, these designs are made up of tiny squares. Each square is the same as one needlepoint stitch.

Use the graph paper to design your own pictures.

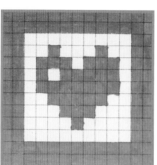

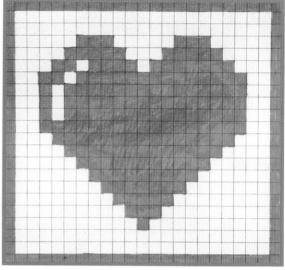

For more stitching patterns, see pages 122—123.

You will need

- Small pieces of canvas
- Tapestry yarn and needle
- Graph paper and pen

How to make a patch

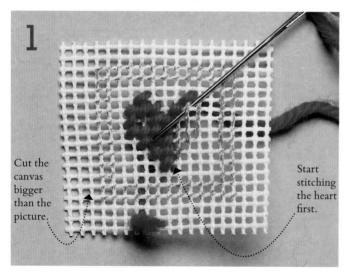

1

Cut the canvas bigger than the picture.

Start stitching the heart first.

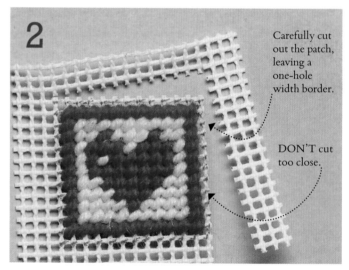

2

Carefully cut out the patch, leaving a one-hole width border.

DON'T cut too close.

3

Stitch over the edge to finish off the patch.

4

You can now use your patch to decorate an item or you can turn it into a badge!

To make a badge, sew a safety pin to a square of felt and glue the felt to your patch.

Handy tip

Your patches can be sewn onto your bags. You can also color-coordinate your patches to match your clothes!

Rainbow frames

Canvas is a strong, stiff material, which makes it ideal for these picture frames. Here is a simple design using bright, rainbow-colored yarn and just one kind of stitch.

You will need

- 10-count canvas
- Tapestry yarn in rainbow colors • Felt for backing • Sewing needle and thread
- Cardboard

How to make a small frame

1 Cut a piece of canvas 5in (12cm) x 5in (12cm).

Cut a hole in the middle, 1½in (3.5cm) x 1½in (3.5cm).

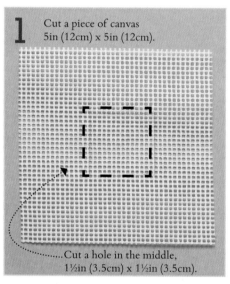

2 Start stitching from the center.

Change color for each row.

Tent stitch

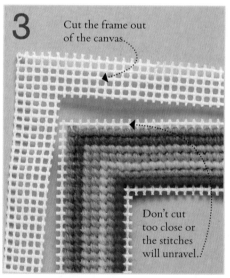

3 Cut the frame out of the canvas.

Don't cut too close or the stitches will unravel.

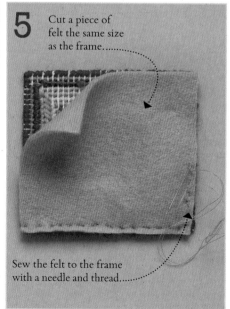

4 Stitch over the rough outer edge.

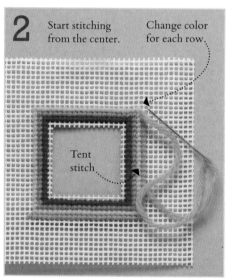

5 Cut a piece of felt the same size as the frame.

Sew the felt to the frame with a needle and thread.

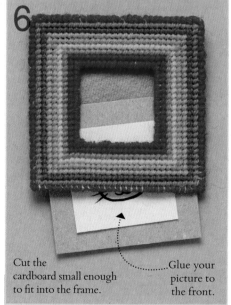

6 Cut the cardboard small enough to fit into the frame.

Glue your picture to the front.

Frame it

Cut larger pieces of canvas, depending on the size of your picture and how much frame you want to stitch. Experiment with different stitches and motifs.

Hang 'em up

Hang your handiwork on the wall with these little tabs. Cut a piece of ribbon and sew it into place on the felt layer of the frame.

Cut a 1½in (4cm) length of ribbon.

Attach with a sewing needle and thread.

Follow the pattern

Center the design on the canvas and use the colored squares to position the stitches and match the colors. Begin stitching the main part of the image first, then work the other colors one at a time.

You will need

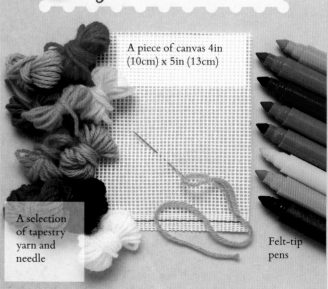

A piece of canvas 4in (10cm) x 5in (13cm)

A selection of tapestry yarn and needle

Felt-tip pens

Pet portraits

Draw a picture of your favorite pet. With some pens and graph paper, turn the portrait into colored squares. No pets? No problem. Stitch these little cats instead. Just use different-colored yarn if you want to change the cat color or background.

Your pet design

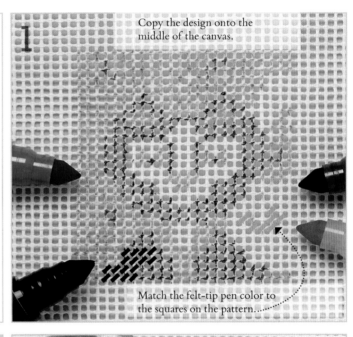

1 Copy the design onto the middle of the canvas.

Match the felt-tip pen color to the squares on the pattern...

2 Begin stitching the main part of the image first, using tent stitch.

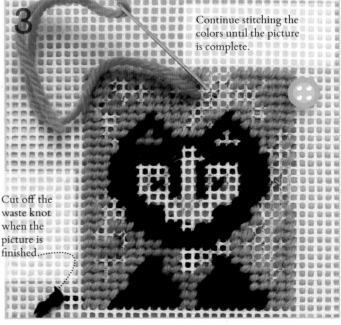

3 Continue stitching the colors until the picture is complete.

Cut off the waste knot when the picture is finished...

Patchwork

Patchwork is made of small pieces of fabric sewn together in geometric patterns to create a large patterned cloth. It's a perfect way to reuse fabric scraps and recycle clothes.

Paper for patches

Each fabric patch will need to be attached to a paper shape. You can reuse old envelopes and magazines to make these. You will need a lot, since each patch requires its own piece of paper. Paper can be reused when the project is finished.

Isometric paper to create designs (see template on pages 120–123)

Tracing paper

Old envelopes work well as paper patches.

Graph paper for patch designs

Sewing needle and pins

Patchwork fabric

Lightweight cotton is best for patchwork; don't use anything stretchy or too thick, since it will be difficult to make the patches even. Experiment with colors and patterns, too.

Sewing thread for basting fabric to paper patches and sewing patches together

Cardboard for templates

Templates

Cardboard from cereal boxes is ideal, but any thin cardboard will do.

Ruler for drawing and measuring templates

Pencil to draw around the shapes

How patchwork works

Every patch needs a piece of fabric and a paper shape. The paper is basted to the fabric, and then these patches are stitched together. The paper remains in the patch until you have finished. Templates made from cardboard are used to get the sizes right for the fabric and paper.

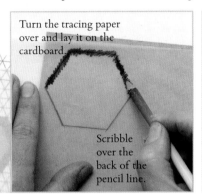

Square   Pentagon   Hexagon   Triangle

Patchwork pieces are based on these shapes.

Copy the shape for the template onto tracing paper using a pencil (see pages 120–121 for templates).

Turn the tracing paper over and lay it on the cardboard.

Scribble over the back of the pencil line.

The pencil line will transfer onto the cardboard.

Templates

Cut out the shapes.

The large shape is for the fabric.

The smaller shape is for the paper.

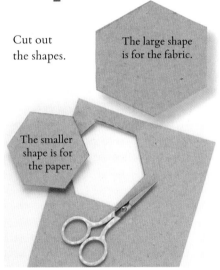

Preparing the paper shapes

1

Carefully draw around the edge.

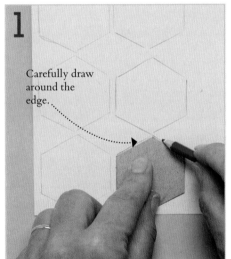

2

Cut out the paper shapes.

It's important to draw and cut the shapes accurately, because they will determine the shape of your final patch.

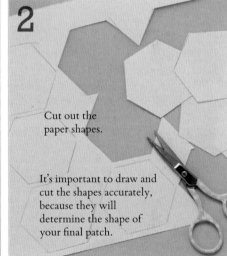

Preparing the fabric

1

Select some fabrics that work well together.

Use the large template for the fabric.

2

Draw around the edge of the cardboard. A ballpoint pen works well on the fabric.

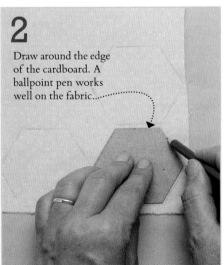

3

Cut out the fabric shapes.

Preparing the patches

1 Fold the fabric over the paper. ......

Carefully pin the paper in the center of the fabric.

REVERSE SIDE OF FABRIC

Hold the fabric in place as you stitch.

2 Use basting stitch to attach the fabric. ......

Stitch over the corner to hold it in place.

3 To finish off, continue stitching to just past the knot.

Remove the pins.

A completed seven-patch block

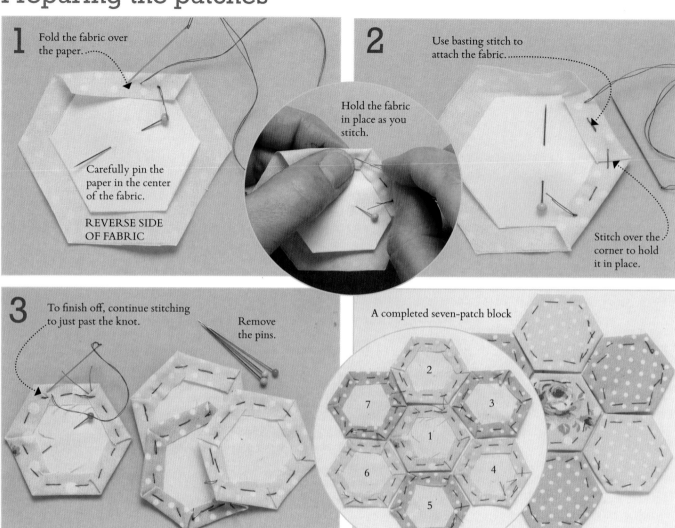

Sewing patches together

1 Place the patches together with their fronts facing each other.

Use tiny stitches to oversew the edges. ......

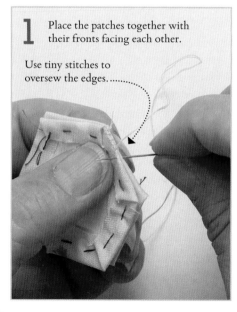

2 At the end of the patch, stitch back over your last few stitches.

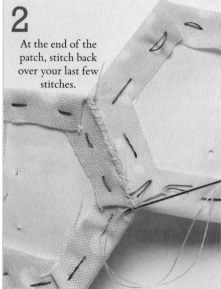

3 Continue stitching the rest of the patches together.

Removing the paper patch

! When all the patches are sewn together, press them flat with an iron.

Cut the basting thread and pull it out.

Carefully remove the paper templates.

Pressing the patch

Once the paper has been removed, the patches are flimsy and the folded seams will tend to unfold. To keep them in shape, press with a hot iron.

! BE CAREFUL—IRONS ARE HOT!

ASK FOR HELP WHEN USING ONE.

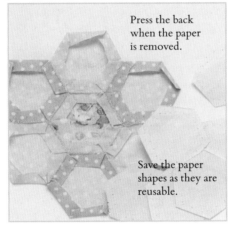

Press the back when the paper is removed.

Save the paper shapes as they are reusable.

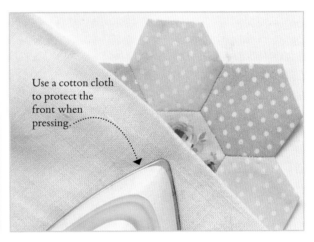

Use a cotton cloth to protect the front when pressing.

Patchwork pattern blocks

Triangles can be used to make up blocks of larger triangles or squares.

Blocks When patches are sewn together like this they are known as blocks. These blocks can help when making large pieces. Placing the blocks in different ways creates all kinds of new designs.

Six-sided shapes, sewn together, make a seven-patch block.

Squares can be joined to make a 9-patch block.

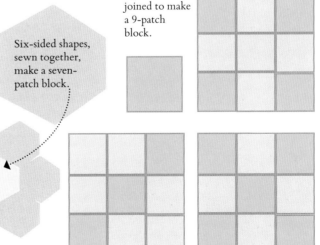

Patchwork squares

Make a comfy quilt for a sleepy toy. This patchwork of squares uses two different fabrics and is one of the easiest designs to put together. Make the squares bigger if you want to create pillows and bags.

How to put the patches together

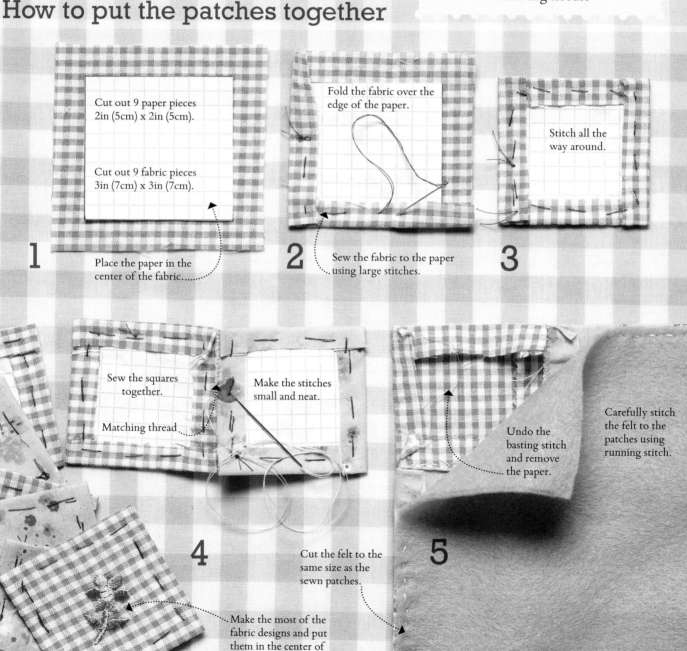

1 Cut out 9 paper pieces 2in (5cm) x 2in (5cm).

Cut out 9 fabric pieces 3in (7cm) x 3in (7cm).

Place the paper in the center of the fabric.

2 Fold the fabric over the edge of the paper.

Sew the fabric to the paper using large stitches.

3 Stitch all the way around.

4 Sew the squares together.

Matching thread

Make the stitches small and neat.

Make the most of the fabric designs and put them in the center of the patch.

5 Undo the basting stitch and remove the paper.

Cut the felt to the same size as the sewn patches.

Carefully stitch the felt to the patches using running stitch.

Z Zz z

Z z z

Handy tip

This design can be used to make pillow covers by making the squares larger. Try 3½in (9cm) x 3½in (9cm) squares.

Squares and triangles

Lots of patterns can be made by placing blocks of triangles in different ways. Choose fabrics with very different contrasting colors and patterns for more dramatic effects.

Make a block

Make four triangular patches using the template on page 120. Try using the graph paper.

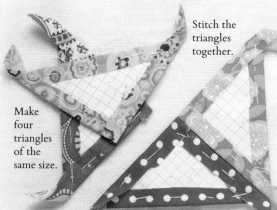

Pin the paper template in the center of the fabric.

Fold the fabric over the paper and sew in place.

You will need

• 4 different fabric designs • Paper templates (see page 120) • Sewing thread and needle

Stitch the triangles together.

Make four triangles of the same size.

Fold down all the pointed ends and pin them along the folded edge. Neatly sew all around the edge.

Make three more blocks in the same way.

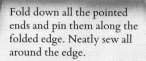

Sew the four blocks together and use an iron to press flat.

Sew blocks together

Turn each block around so the triangles match up differently.

Remove the paper and use an iron to press the reverse side flat.

Project idea

This design has been used to decorate a pillow. Place the block design centrally on the pillow and sew it on neatly. If you sew lots of blocks together you can make a big floor pillow.

Patchy pillows

Shaped like honeycombs, these six-sided patches are sewn together to make a seven-patch block. Here, two blocks have been stitched together and stuffed to make pillows.

Make 2 seven-patch blocks

To make the blocks, follow the steps on pages 50–53.

This design uses a different fabric for each patch.

To help flatten the fabric, iron the blocks before removing the paper.

How to make a pin pillow

1 Remove the template paper.

...Iron the fabric edges flat again at this stage.

2 Place the blocks with the wrong sides facing each other.

Neatly oversew the edges together.

Leave an opening for the filling.

3 Fill the pillow, working the stuffing into the corners...

Neatly sew up the opening.

Little and Large

It's so simple;
the size of the patch will
make a smaller or larger
pillow. Go to pages 120–123
and try out some different
templates.

Match the patch

The seven-patch
blocks can be sewn together
to become a larger piece of
fabric, such as a quilt for
your bed.

Five-sided patches

Take 12 patches, stitch them together and, as if by magic, they form to make a charming soft ball— the perfect present for a baby. Cat lovers, too, can pamper their pets with these toys by adding a little catnip to the stuffing. They'll have happy cats, indeed!

Handy tip
The template shown is for the smaller ball. To make the larger ball, increase the size of the template.

Did you know?
A 12-sided object is called a **dodecahedron**—who would have guessed these pretty patchwork balls would have such a serious name! A five-sided shape is a **pentagon.**

You will need
• Variety of lightweight fabric, such as cotton
• Cardboard and paper template • Sewing needle
• Sewing thread, matching and contrasting colors • Soft-toy filling

Five-sided template

Two sizes Cut the large shape out of cardboard, and the small shape from paper.

Trace over the shape. Cut a piece of thin cardboard to the large size; cut the small size from paper.

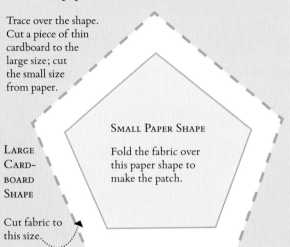

LARGE CARD- BOARD SHAPE

Cut fabric to this size.....

SMALL PAPER SHAPE

Fold the fabric over this paper shape to make the patch.

A flower shape

Six patches sewn together

.....Basting stitches hold the backing paper in place.

Patchy decoration

If you like the flower shape, you can use it as a decorative motif. Remove the paper templates before stitching it in place. Here, it's sewn to the front of a bag.

Patch match

For a really fancy ball, choose at least six different fabrics. Pick them carefully—they don't have to match, but they do need to look good together.

Dark sewing thread for the basting stitches.....

Sewing thread to match the fabric.....

Sewing needle.....

x - x - x - x - x - x - x - x - x - x - x - x - x - x - x - x - x - x - x -

How to make patchwork balls

You will need 12 five-sided patches. Stitch the patches together as shown below and make two cup shapes. Match up the cups and stitch them together, leaving an opening for the stuffing.

Arrange the patches so each patch is next to a different fabric.

Draw around the cardboard template.

Cut out 12 fabric pieces.

Place the paper template in the center.

Use a different colored thread.

Baste the fabric over the edge of the paper.

Make a flower shape x 2

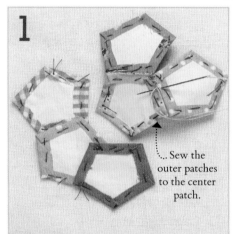

1

...Sew the outer patches to the center patch.

2

Repeat step 1 to create another flower shape like this.

3

Sew together the sides of the outer patches.

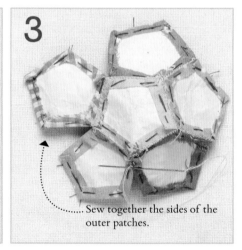

4

When all the sides are sewn up, they will form a cup shape.

To achieve the ball shape, join the two cups together by matching the tips of the patches on one of the cups into the "V"-shaped space on the other.

5 Make two cup shapes

Place this point into the "V" shape of the other cup.

x - x - x - x - x - x - x - x - x - x - x - x - x - x - x - x - x - x - x -

Stitch the two cups together

1 Stitch the patches together.

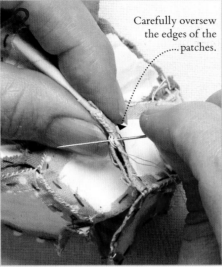

Carefully oversew the edges of the patches.

3 Leave an opening to allow for the filling.

Form a ball

1 Remove the basting stitches.

Discard the paper templates.

2 Turn the ball inside out.

3 Stuff the ball until it feels firm, not squishy.

Finish the ball

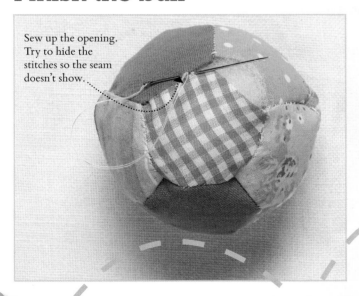

Sew up the opening. Try to hide the stitches so the seam doesn't show.

Pretty puffs

These dainty puffed shapes are simply made from circles of cotton fabric gathered up tight—puffect!

Puff necklace

Create a garland of puffs by sewing them together. Add buttons to the middles and ribbon for ties.

Join the puffs together.

Decorate the puffs with buttons.

Make a Puff

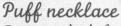

You will need

- A circular template 6in (15cm) across
- Scraps of cotton fabric
- Sewing needle and thread
- Ballpoint pen

1 Using a bowl as a template, draw around the edge.

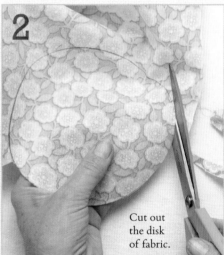

2 Cut out the disk of fabric.

3 Fold over ¼in (7mm) of the fabric edge and hem.

Use a loose running stitch to sew around the edge.

4 Once the hem is stitched, gently pull the thread to gather up the fabric.

5 Work the fabric around to make the gathers even.

Sew a couple of stitches to secure the gathers.

Join them up

Puffs are a traditional patchwork technique. Try joining lots of puffs together to make a cover for a plain pillow or join even more together and make a colorful bed throw.

Carefully sew through the edges of the puffs.

Appliqué

What is appliqué? Well, it's pictures and patterns made by sewing small fabric shapes to a piece of material. Motifs can be used like patches to dress up clothing. Sewing stitches can be invisible, but embroidery stitches are a perfect way to add decoration.

Tracing paper

Fabrics

Lightweight cotton fabric is best for appliqué. In addition to coming in an array of colors and patterns, it is easy to cut and shape. The cut edges will fray, but stitching the edges and using adhesive transfer paper will help. Avoid stretchy fabric, since this can distort the motif shapes.

Buttons for decoration

Tracing paper

Use this for copying an image and transferring the outline as a pattern for your piece of fabric.

Transfer paper

Transfer paper

Used in dressmaking and craft projects, this paper has a glued backing that, when heated, can be used to attach motifs to the fabric items.

Embroidery thread

Needles and pins

Sewing thread

Scissors for cutting out shapes

Felt fabric

Felt will not fray like other fabrics because of the way it is made. This makes it ideal for appliqué, since even the smallest motifs will keep their shape.

Pencil for tracing motifs

Transferring designs using transfer paper

What is transfer paper?

Transfer paper is a handy way to attach motifs to the fabric items you want to decorate. It's like tracing paper with glue on one side. It works in two steps; first you stick the paper shape to your motif fabric and then you iron the motif to the fabric you are decorating. Follow the manufacturer's instructions.

1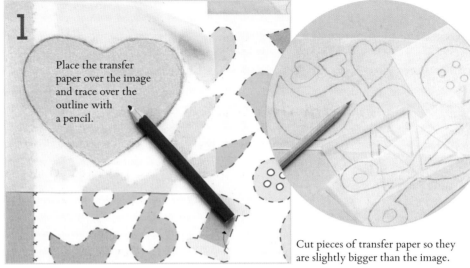

Place the transfer paper over the image and trace over the outline with a pencil.

Cut pieces of transfer paper so they are slightly bigger than the image.

2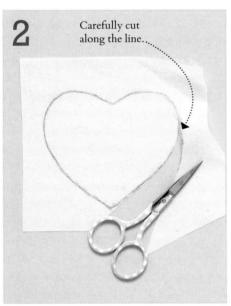

Carefully cut along the line.

3

Place the paper shape on the wrong side of the fabric.

Gently iron over the paper shape until it is fixed in place.

!

4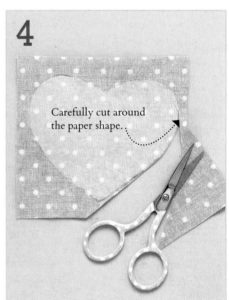

Carefully cut around the paper shape.

5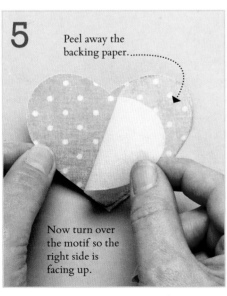

Peel away the backing paper.

Now turn over the motif so the right side is facing up.

6

Carefully position the motif where you want it to go.

Gently iron all over the motif until it is stuck down.

!

Using an iron

!

CAREFUL—IRONS ARE HOT!

ASK FOR HELP IF USING ONE.

- The iron will need to be hot to make the transfer paper work effectively.
- PLEASE NOTE: Some fabrics will melt if you iron them. Place a piece of cotton cloth over the fabric motif before ironing to prevent this from happening.

Paper patterns

Fabric motifs can be attached by simply pinning them directly to the base fabric. Trace over the image and cut out the shape, then, using the tracing-paper shape, cut out the fabric motif.

Tracing paper template

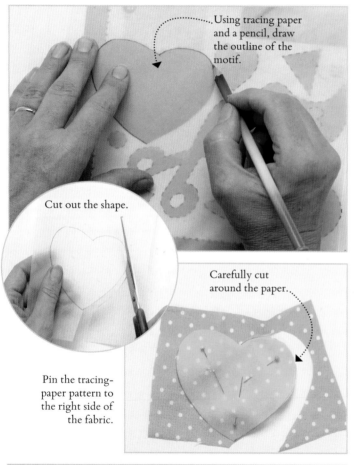

Using tracing paper and a pencil, draw the outline of the motif.

Cut out the shape.

Carefully cut around the paper.

Pin the tracing-paper pattern to the right side of the fabric.

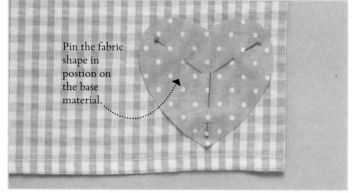

Pin the fabric shape in postion on the base material.

Decorative stitching

Stitches used for attaching the motifs can be tiny and invisible, using sewing thread, or they can be made to be part of the design. Try using the stitches from the Embroidery pages of the book (pages 14–35). Here are three decorative ways of making stitches part of the design using embroidery thread.

RUNNING STITCH

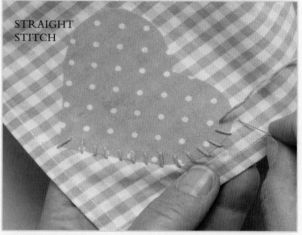

STRAIGHT STITCH

BLANKET STITCH

This stitch is useful if the edges of fabric are fraying.

Ready-made motifs

Look for fabric with big, bold designs because these make perfect motifs.

Custom designs

Design your own motifs. If you can't find a design you like or you have a picture in mind, draw the design on paper and use this as your pattern. Cut out the shapes and pin them to the fabric, then cut out to make the fabric shapes.

Handy tip

If you don't have any adhesive transfer paper, simply cut out the shapes, pin them to the backing material, and sew them in place.

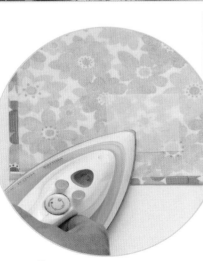

! Iron the paper on the reverse of the fabric, over the motif.

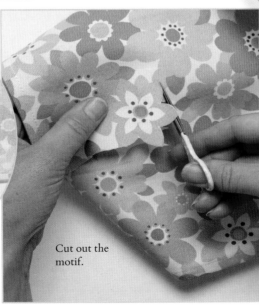

Cut out the motif.

! Iron the motif in position.

Cupcake bag

Create a delicious cupcake bag made of felt and buttons. First, draw your design on paper, then cut it out to use as the pattern. Felt is great because it doesn't fray at the edges.

You will need

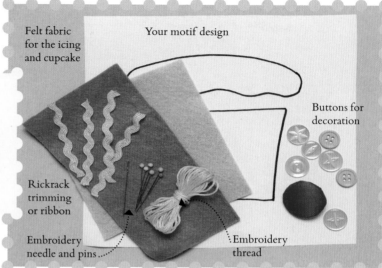

Felt fabric for the icing and cupcake

Your motif design

Buttons for decoration

Rickrack trimming or ribbon

Embroidery needle and pins

Embroidery thread

Bag size

Cut out a piece of fabric 8in (20cm) x 16in (40cm). Position the motif in the top half of the fabric, as shown below. Remember to allow space for the seams and for folding down edges at the top of the bag.

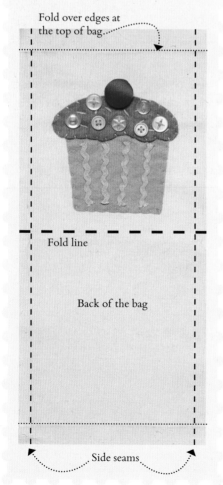

Fold over edges at the top of bag

Fold line

Back of the bag

Side seams

How to make the motif

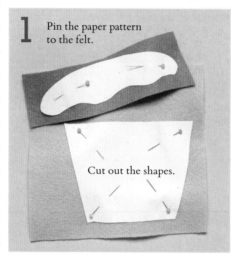

1 Pin the paper pattern to the felt.

Cut out the shapes.

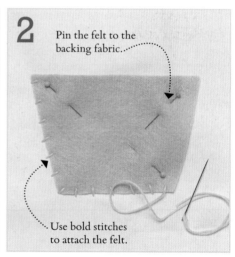

2 Pin the felt to the backing fabric.

Use bold stitches to attach the felt.

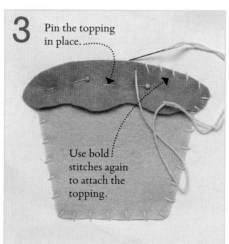

3 Pin the topping in place.

Use bold stitches again to attach the topping.

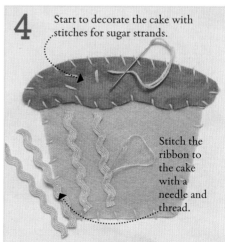

4 Start to decorate the cake with stitches for sugar strands.

Stitch the ribbon to the cake with a needle and thread.

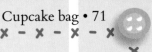

If you already have a bag, why not decorate that instead? Just follow the motif step-by-steps in the same way.

Use ribbon to look like the sides of a baking cup.

Collect buttons to decorate your work.

Make a bag

Fold the fabric in half, right sides facing. Fold the tops of the bag over and stitch in place on either side. Sew together the sides using backstitch. Finally, pin the handles on and sew them in position (see pages 118–119 for more bags).

Fold over the fabric at the top and sew up the sides.

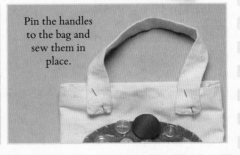

Pin the handles to the bag and sew them in place.

Mmm... doughnuts

Which flavor to make? Chocolate or plain? It's easy to do—just change the felt color. Appliqué the icing, then finish your doughnuts with a sprinkle of stitches. They will look good enough to eat!

Cut out a template

Cut out two circles of felt for the doughnut.....

Cut out one piece of colored felt for the icing.......

How to make a doughnut

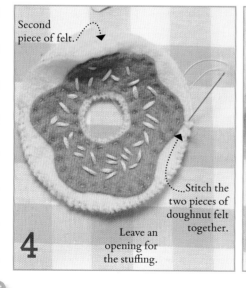

Felt shapes for doughnut and icing.

Needles and thread for sewing and embroidery

1 You'll need some stuffing fiber, too.

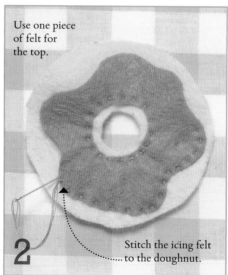

Use one piece of felt for the top.

2 Stitch the icing felt to the doughnut.

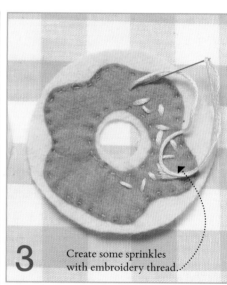

3 Create some sprinkles with embroidery thread.

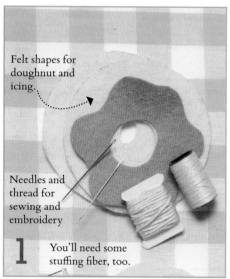

Second piece of felt.

4 Stitch the two pieces of doughnut felt together. Leave an opening for the stuffing.

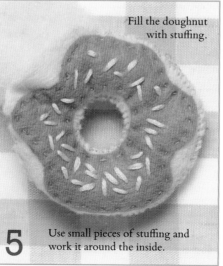

Fill the doughnut with stuffing.

5 Use small pieces of stuffing and work it around the inside.

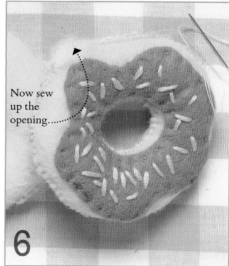

Now sew up the opening.

6

Handy tip

To help get the stuffing to go all the way around the doughnut try gently pushing it into place with a blunt pencil—but don't push too hard, or you'll go through the stitching.

Sprinkles of stitches

Try a mix of colors to give the effect of sugar strands and sprinkles. Try adding beads for a 3-D effect.

Birds, bunting, and buttons

Make beautiful craft boxes.
Using even the smallest scraps of fabric, appliqué is a perfect way to create patches to decorate boxes and bags. These sewing theme motifs make a lovely finish to your craft kit.

You will need

• Adhesive transfer paper •
Pencil • Iron • Backing
fabric • Scraps of fabric for
shapes • Sewing thread
and needle

Trace the shapes from this page onto the transfer paper.

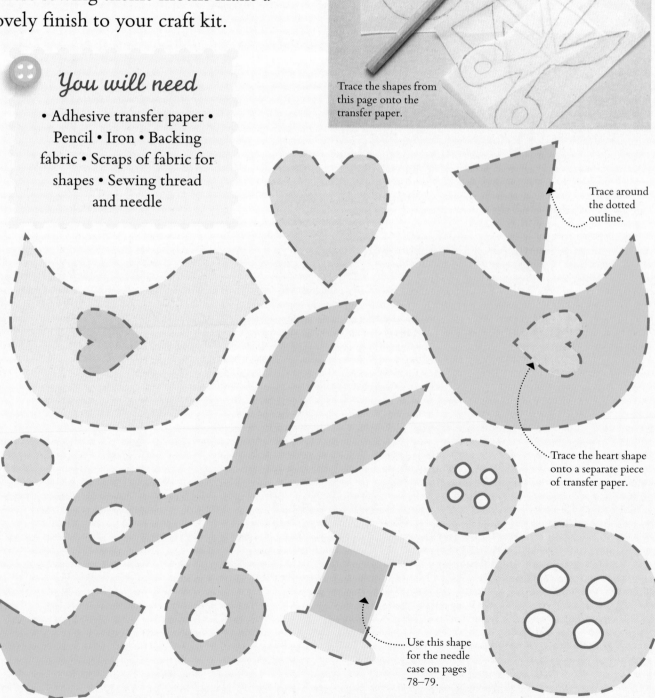

Trace around the dotted outline.

Trace the heart shape onto a separate piece of transfer paper.

Use this shape for the needle case on pages 78–79.

x - x - x - x - x - x - x - x - x - x - x - x - x - x - x - x - x - x - x - x - x - x -

Position the shapes

WARNING: THE IRON IS HOT!

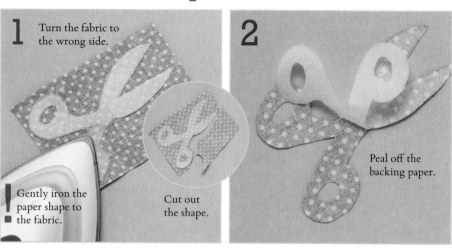

1 Turn the fabric to the wrong side.

! Gently iron the paper shape to the fabric.

Cut out the shape.

2 Peal off the backing paper.

3 Place the shape right-side up on the fabric.

! Gently iron the shape onto the fabric.

Scissor design

Collect up all the pieces you want to decorate the fabric patch. The rickrack border and very small scraps of fabric do not need the adhesive backing.

Sew the shape to the fabric patch with running stitch.

The stitches are for decoration, so keep them neat and even.

Small shapes and buttons can be sewn directly onto the patch.

Position the rickrack with pins, then sew in place.

Match the ends of the rickrack, so they are neat.

Carefully snip holes for the fabric buttons.

Sew the buttons on with different-colored thread.

Birds and bunting

Cut out a piece of fabric for the patch.

Cut out the fabric shapes.

Prepare the shapes to be ironed on.

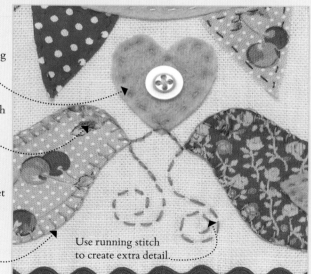

Make a feature of the running stitches.

Use French knots for the eyes.

Use blanket stitch for a decorative edge.

Use running stitch to create extra detail.

x - x - x - x - x - x - x - x - x - x - x - x - x - x - x - x - x - x - x - x - x - x - x

Pin cushion

This big-button motif makes a pretty pin cushion or button-box lid.

Craft in a bag

Here a patch has been sewn onto a small tote bag—a handy place to keep your craft materials.

More ideas
The finished patches can be applied to all kinds of surfaces. Either stitch them onto fabric like this bag or glue them onto a box lid.

Big-button design

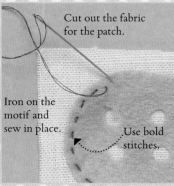

Cut out the fabric for the patch.

Iron on the motif and sew in place.

Use bold stitches.

Finish it off with a rickrack border.

Needle case

Keep all your pins and needles on hand in a simple cloth case. This design helps you practice your sewing skills— sewing buttons and appliqué.

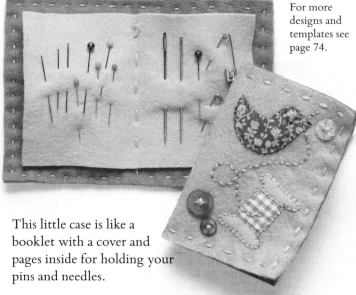

For more designs and templates see page 74.

This little case is like a booklet with a cover and pages inside for holding your pins and needles.

You will need

Cut out fabric bird shape and bobbin

Sewing needle and embroidery needle

For the cover: Cut out two pieces of fabric 5½in (14.5cm) x 4in (10.5cm).

For the inside: Cut out one piece of fabric 5in (12cm) x 3½in (9cm).

Embroidery thread

Sewing thread

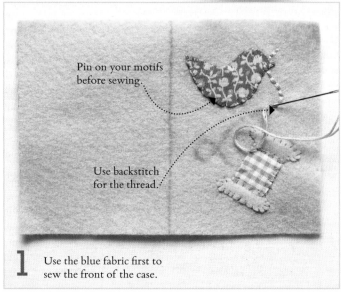

Pin on your motifs before sewing.

Use backstitch for the thread.

1 Use the blue fabric first to sew the front of the case.

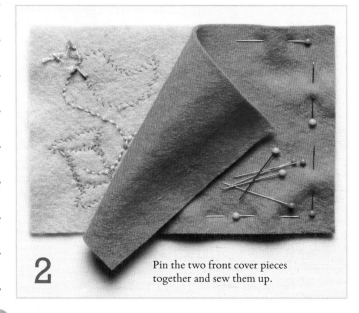

2 Pin the two front cover pieces together and sew them up.

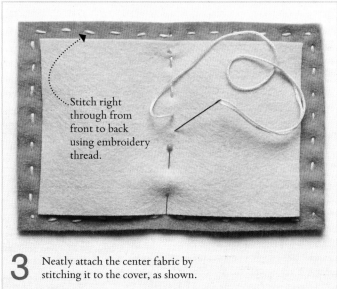

Stitch right through from front to back using embroidery thread.

3 Neatly attach the center fabric by stitching it to the cover, as shown.

Ready-made

Patterned fabrics are perfect places to find ready-made motifs. Simply cut out an image and sew with embroidery stitches to decorate your wardrobe.

Draw a heart shape around the image and cut it out.

Attach the heart motif with blanket stitch.

Sweetheart

This cute little motif has been made by selecting an area on a piece a fabric, drawing a heart shape to frame the image, then cutting it out and sewing it in place.

Flower shapes

Select a motif and iron on the adhesive transfer paper.

Select the flower you want and either use the iron-on method to attach it to the backing fabric or sew it directly into position. Use embroidery stitches (see pages 16–18) to decorate the flower. Work in contrasting colors and add buttons for extra decoration.

Stitch crazy

Cut out the shapes and attach them to your clothes, then go wild with the stitching. Transform a simple flower design into something stunning.

Tiny pictures make perfect little patches. Frame in blanket stitch with colorful embroidery thread.

You can also attach motifs with transfer paper. Trace around your motif onto the paper to cut out. Stick down and iron.

Decorate with a variety of embroidery stitches and add a button in the middle.

Knitting

Two needles and a ball of yarn are all you need to start knitting. Work the stitches from one needle to the other and see the fabric grow.

KNITTING RULES
There are no set rules about how to use the yarn and needles—knitters all around the world use them in very different ways. The following pages show two methods, one of which is preferred by left-handed knitters.

Knitting needles

Knitting needles are available in many different sizes, from very narrow ones for fine work to very thick ones that produce a bulky knit. The projects that follow use a medium-sized needle.

Tapestry needle for sewing up projects

Knitting spool

Also known as a Knitting Nancy and French Knitting, this gadget knits yarn into long braids that can be used with all kinds of projects.

The pin is used to work the yarn over the top of hooks on the spool.

Size 6 (4mm) knitting needles

Stitch types

There are two stitch types used in the projects that follow: "Knit stitch" and "Purl stitch." Knitting patterns shorten the names as shown below:
K = knit
P = purl
st = stitch

Braids made with the knitting spool.

DK yarn

Yarns

The many different types of yarn are described by their "weight." The yarn used for the projects that follow is a double knit or DK weight and made of either wool or acrylic. Other yarns are known as 4-ply and bulky. Each yarn will produce a different feel to the fabric.

How to get started

Knitting is produced with two needles, one held in each hand. To begin, you need to make stitches—this is called "casting on." You will need to cast on the number of stitches required in the pattern. The stitches that are being worked will be on the left-hand needle and the ones you have made will go on the right.

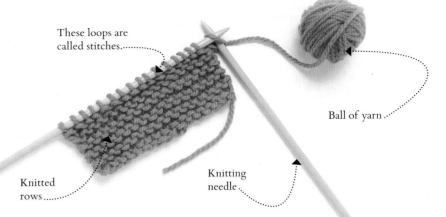

These loops are called stitches

Ball of yarn

Knitted rows

Knitting needle

Slip knot
The first stitch on the needle is knotted so the yarn stays on.

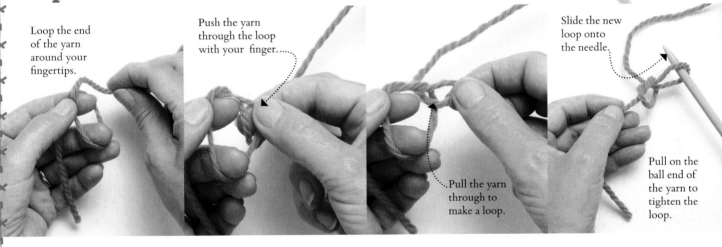

Loop the end of the yarn around your fingertips.

Push the yarn through the loop with your finger.

Pull the yarn through to make a loop.

Slide the new loop onto the needle.

Pull on the ball end of the yarn to tighten the loop.

Casting on
There are many ways to cast on. This method uses your thumb.

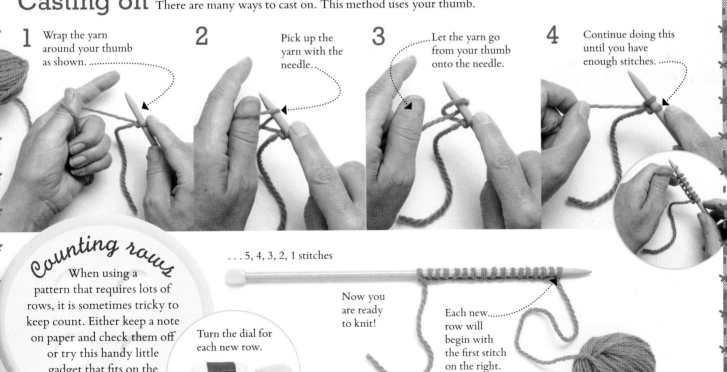

1 Wrap the yarn around your thumb as shown.

2 Pick up the yarn with the needle.

3 Let the yarn go from your thumb onto the needle.

4 Continue doing this until you have enough stitches.

Counting rows
When using a pattern that requires lots of rows, it is sometimes tricky to keep count. Either keep a note on paper and check them off or try this handy little gadget that fits on the end of your needle.

Turn the dial for each new row.

. . . 5, 4, 3, 2, 1 stitches

Now you are ready to knit!

Each new row will begin with the first stitch on the right.

Knit Stitch

Also called plain stitch, this stitch is generally thought to be the easiest to make and is certainly a useful basic stitch for simple projects.

For knit stitch, the right-hand needle goes to the back of the stitch.

The yarn also goes at the back.

Method 1   (This is called the "English" method.)

1 Hold the knitting with your hands in this position.

Place the needle in the back of the stitch.

Take the yarn around the back.

2 Wrap the yarn under and around the needle from right to left.

Method 2   (This is called the "Continental" method; it is sometimes preferred by left-hander knitters.)

1 Place the yarn between the fingers of your left hand.

2 Use your middle finger to move the yarn.

Your index finger and thumb are used to hold the knitting in place.

Take the yarn around the front of the needle.

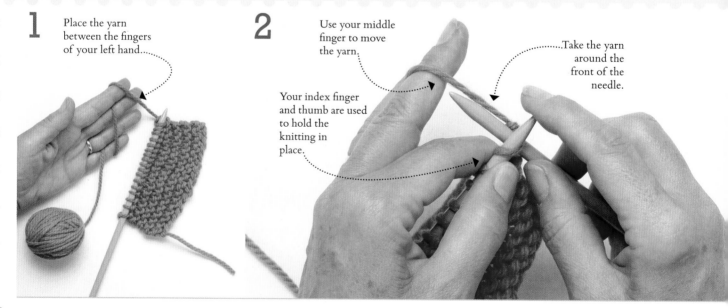

Garter Stitch

Garter stitch isn't an actual stitch but the name given to a piece of knitting where every row is knitted in knit stitch. The effect is bumpy on both sides.

Garter stitch is also made if you knit every row in purl stitch.

3 Pull on the yarn and move the needle from the back to the front.

4 The right needle is now on top of the left one and has taken the stitch with it.

5 Slide the top needle to the right. The stitch will now be transferred onto the right needle, completing the stitch.

Begin the next stitch as in step 1.

3 Bring the yarn down firmly between the needles.

4 Bring the needle with the loop of yarn to the front.

Push the stitch along the needle.

5 Take the needle with the stitch off the left-hand needle.

Begin the next stitch as in step 1.

Making shapes

You can shape the knitting by adding (increasing) or taking away (decreasing) stitches. There are many different ways to do this, but here are two simple methods that you can use for the projects in this book.

INCREASE SHAPE

...An extra stitch has been made at the beginning and the end of each row.

Two stitches have been knitted together at the beginning and end of each row.

DECREASE SHAPE

Make a stitch—increasing

1 Begin a knit stitch as normal.

2 Don't remove the stitch from the needle.

3 Take the right-hand needle behind the left needle.

Back of stitch

4 Place the needle into the back of the stitch.

5 Bring the yarn around and knit in the normal way.

6 Pull the yarn between the needles...

...7 Bring the right-hand needle to the front, carrying the new stitch with it.

8 Remove the rest of the stitch off the left-hand needle.

...The new stitch.

Knit two together—decreasing

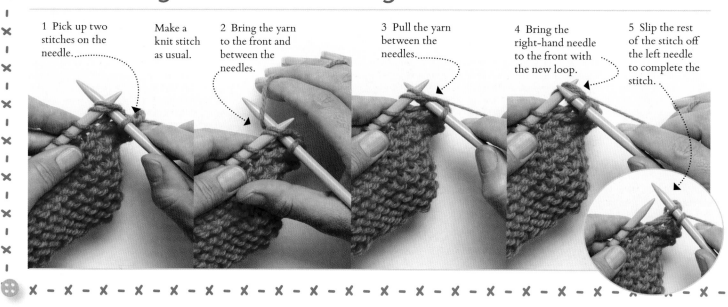

1 Pick up two stitches on the needle...

Make a knit stitch as usual.

2 Bring the yarn to the front and between the needles.

3 Pull the yarn between the needles...

4 Bring the right-hand needle to the front with the new loop.

5 Slip the rest of the stitch off the left needle to complete the stitch.

Join new yarn

1 Tie the new yarn to the old yarn with a loose knot.

2 Slide the knot up the yarn to the needle.

3 Continue knitting as usual.

Knit in new color

Here, the knitting is shown on the reverse side. Join the new yarn as shown (left). To neaten the loose ends of both colors, gather them up with the working yarn as you knit.

Casting off

1 Begin the row by knitting two stitches...

2 Pick up the first stitch with the left needle.

3 Carry this first stitch over the second stitch and over the end of the needle...

4 Repeat steps 1–3...

5 ... until one stitch remains. Open up the loop.

6 Cut the yarn and place the end in the loop.

7 Pull the yarn to close the loop.

Neaten up ends (Sewing in ends when adding new yarn or neatening the loose ends of finished pieces).

Use this method when neatening up joined yarn and when knitting stripes.

Thread the end with an embroidery needle.

Sew the thread into the edge of the knitting.

Bring the needle out and cut the yarn.

Use this method when neatening loose ends of finished pieces.

Thread the needle onto the loose end and sew down the side of the knitting.

Bring the needle out and cut the yarn.

Just knit it!

Master knit stitch and you can make plenty of things just by using one stitch. Here's a chance for you to practice your skills.

You will need

- Size 6 (4mm) knitting needles • DK yarn

HAT
2 x 50-gm
balls

SCARF
2 x 50-gm
balls

BAG
1 x 50-gm
ball

STRAP
1 x 50-gm
ball

RIBBON
1 x 50-gm
ball

Hat

Cast on 50 stitches. Row 1 knit stitch. Continue using knit stitch until the piece measures 16in (40cm). Cast off.

Scarf

Cast on 24 stitches. Row 1 knit stitch. Continue using knit stitch until the scarf measures 36in (90cm). Cast off.

Bag

Cast on 14 stitches. Row 1 knit stitch. Continue using knit stitch until your piece measures 10in (24cm). Cast off.

Bag strap

Cast on 3 stitches. Row 1 knit stitch. Continue using knit stitch until the strap measures 30in (76cm). Cast off.

Ribbon

Cast on 6 stitches. Row 1 knit stitch. Continue using knit stitch until the ribbon measures 16in (40cm). Cast off.

HAT

SCARF

RIBBON

BAG
STRAP

BAG

Button up

These plain knits can be easily brightened up—try adding colorful buttons or mix up the colors by adding a multicolored fringe to your scarf.

How to make hats, scarves, bags, and bows

Start by sewing the loose ends into the pieces of knitting (see page 87). Use a tapestry needle and the yarn that you used to make the item to sew the pieces together. When you have finished, use buttons to decorate the pieces.

Pass it along the edge of the knitting.

Thread the end on to a needle.

Pass the yarn along the edge of the knitting.

Make a hat

Fold the knitting in half.

Place the edges together.

Pin in place and begin to sew.

Turn the hat inside out and fold up the edge to make the hat smaller.

Make a bag

Fold the knitting in half.

Pin the sides together.

Stitch together with backstitch.

Attach the strap to the edge of the bag.

Making tassels

The thickness of the tassel can vary, depending on how many loops of yarn you make. Cut a piece of cardboard twice the length you'd like your tassels to be. Tie the yarn to the cardboard and wind it around 8 times. Cut the yarn at the top and bottom. To make a tassel, take two strands and fold them in half.

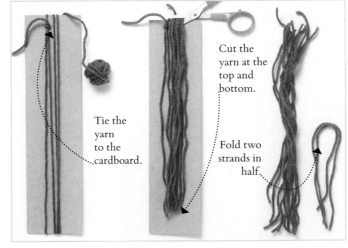

Tie the yarn to the cardboard.

Cut the yarn at the top and bottom.

Fold two strands in half.

1 Push a large crochet hook through the edge of the knitting...

Hook up the two folded strands of yarn.

2 Carefully take the hook back through the knitting, pulling the yarn with it....

3 Remove the hook.

4 Place the yarn ends through the loop to create a loose knot....

5 Space the tassels evenly across the end of the scarf.

Cut the tassels to the same length when they are all in place.

Make a bow

You can also simply tie your ribbon into a bow.

Fold one end over across the middle.....

Fold the other end over across the first....

Sew in place with a few stitches...

Purl stitch

It's all front with purl stitch. The yarn is worked from the front and the needle goes in the front of the stitch.

For purl stitch, the needle goes in the front of the stitch.

The yarn also goes at the front, too.

Method 1 (The "English" method)

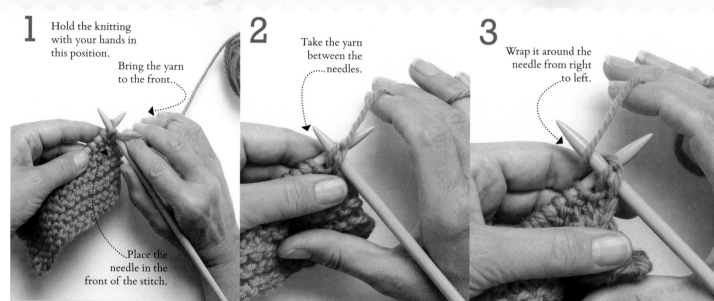

1 Hold the knitting with your hands in this position.

Bring the yarn to the front.

Place the needle in the front of the stitch.

2 Take the yarn between the needles.

3 Wrap it around the needle from right to left.

Method 2 (The "Continental" method; left-hander knitters might find this method helpful.)

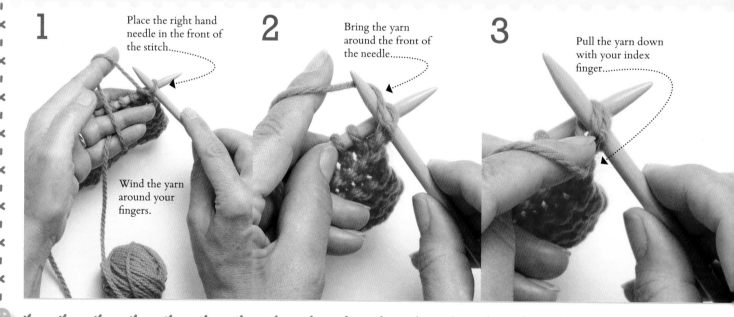

1 Place the right hand needle in the front of the stitch.

Wind the yarn around your fingers.

2 Bring the yarn around the front of the needle.

3 Pull the yarn down with your index finger.

Purl stitch + Knit stitch = Stockinette stitch

STOCKINETTE STITCH isn't an actual stitch at all. Instead, it is made by working a knit row then a purl row, a knit row then a purl row, and so on. The result is a smooth front to the knitting and a "knobby" back.

FRONT
The knit-stitch side

BACK
The purl-stitch side

4 Pull on the yarn and move the needle from front to back...

5 ... taking the stitch with it...

6 Take the rest of the yarn off the needle to complete the stitch...

Begin the next stitch as in step 1.

4 Bring the right-hand needle from front to back taking the yarn with it......

5 Pull the rest of the stitch off the needle...

6 Now you are ready to begin the next stitch, starting at Step 1 again.

Dude dolls

Make an all-in-one doll. Begin by knitting a striped rectangle. In a few simple steps, transform it into a little knitted man.

You will need

- Knitting needles Size 6 (4mm)
- 4 balls of yarn • soft-toy stuffing
- Tapestry needle

Stop here! Cast off.

Get started
Work from the bottom, changing yarn color as you move up so that each stripe represents a part of the doll's body.

Start here! Cast on 32 stitches.

Hat
Work 10 rows · This color is part of the 10 rows for the hat

Head
Work 10 rows—change yarn

Sweater
Work 12 rows—change yarn

Pants
Work 14 rows—change yarn

Shoes
Work 4 rows—change yarn

Work from shoes to hat.

Add felt dots for eyes.

How to make the doll

1

Fold the knitting in half so it's inside out.

Sew the edges together.

2

Sew around the top of the knitting and gather it up.

3

Turn the work right-side out.

Add the stuffing and sew up the opening.

4

To form the head, sew in a running stitch around the base of the head stripe.

5

Firmly pull on the thread to create a neck.

Add a stitch to make it secure.

6

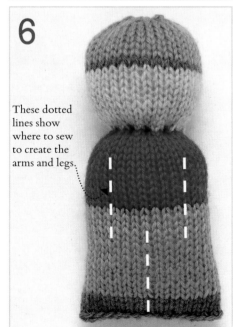

These dotted lines show where to sew to create the arms and legs.

7

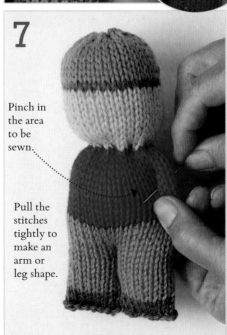

Pinch in the area to be sewn.

Pull the stitches tightly to make an arm or leg shape.

Knitted roses

Make a bunch of colorful woolly roses. These simple knitted shapes are twisted and curled to form a rose flower. It only takes a small amount of yarn to make one, so it's a neat way to use up leftover yarn.

You will need

Size 6 (4mm) knitting needles • 15ft (5m) of yarn • Felt • Embroidery needle • Sewing needle and thread

Rose pattern

Cast on 32 stitches
Row 1: Knit st
Row 2: Purl st
Row 3: Knit st
Row 4: Purl st
Decrease
Row 5: knit two together to end of row =16 st
Row 6: knit two together to end of row = 8 st
Row 7: knit two together to end of row = 4 st
Row 8: knit two together = 2 st
Cast off

How to make a rose

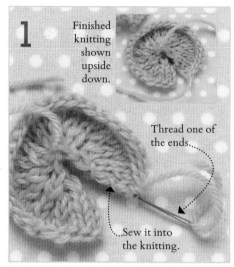

1 Finished knitting shown upside down.

Thread one of the ends.

Sew it into the knitting.

2 Thread the yarn end from the center.

3 Turn over the knitting.

Twist the knitting into a tight curl to form the rose shape.

4 Sew the outer side of the curl to the back of the rose to hold it in position.

5 Cut out some felt leaves.

Sew the leaf to the back of the rose.

Overstitch the edge of the felt with small neat stitches.

Rosy brooch

Your rose makes a pretty brooch. Sew a safety pin to the felt leaves, or sew the roses directly onto your bags, either on their own or in bunches of three.

x - x - x - x - x - x - x - x - x - x - x - x - x - x - x - x - x - x - x - x - x - x -

Knitting braids

Knit some string.

Once you get the hang of it, using a knitting spool is a lot of fun.

You will need

• A variety of colorful knitting yarn (DK weight is good) • Knitting spool with pin

How to get started

Thread the yarn through the top of the spool.

Turn the yarn around the first hook...

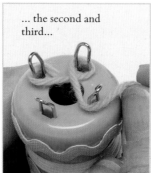

... the second and third...

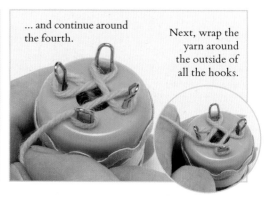

... and continue around the fourth.

Next, wrap the yarn around the outside of all the hooks.

Making stitches

Use the pin to pull out the loop.

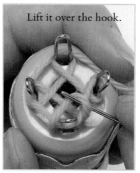

Lift it over the hook.

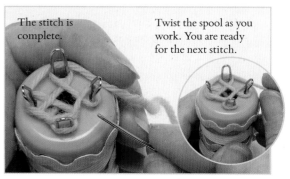

The stitch is complete.

Twist the spool as you work. You are ready for the next stitch.

Casting off

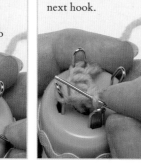

Take the first stitch off the hook and place it over the hook to the left to make a stitch.

Lift the stitch to the next hook.

Make the last stitch.

Lift up the last stitch and enlarge the loop.

Cut the yarn, thread it through the hoop, and pull to finish.

x - x - x - x - x - x - x - x - x - x - x - x - x - x - x - x - x - x - x - x - x - x - x

Use long braids about 12in (30cm).

Fold the braid backward and forward.

Sew the two pieces together....

Loopy rose

Add green braids to make the leaves.

Things to make

Braids can be turned into all kinds of fun designs. Try these flower shapes (if you sew on a safety pin you can turn them into brooches).

Tuck the ends away.

Use about 10 braids 8in (20cm) long.........

Tie the braids together tightly at the middle.........

Daisy flower

Curl up a braid and sew it to the middle of the bunch.........

Thread the long end on to a needle and thread it down through the braid 1¼in (3cm). Pull the needle out and cut off the yarn.

Handy tip

Hold the spool in your left hand and use the pin in the right hand. Twist the spool as you work so the next stitch is facing you. Remember, don't knit too tightly.

As the braid grows, pull the end to tighten the work at the top.

Dangly legs and arms

Make us and our dangly arms and legs (see pages 100–103).

The lollipop dolls

Knit a doll, then have fun dressing her and styling her hair. Made up of separate parts, the doll's body is in two colors with a stripe of body color at the top that makes a ready-made bodice. Her cute, dangly legs are made using a knitting spool.

You will need

• Size 6 (4mm) knitting needles
• Knitting spool • 3ft (1m) yarn for body • 3ft (1m) for skirt
• 20in (50cm) yarn for bodice
• 3ft (1m) yarn for hair
• Knitting spool

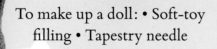

To make up a doll: • Soft-toy filling • Tapestry needle

Basic doll pattern

Head • Making the ball shape involves increasing and decreasing. It's the trickiest part of the pattern.
Body and bodice • Make in two colors so it looks like the doll is already wearing clothes.
Arms and Legs • Use the body color yarn and a knitting spool.

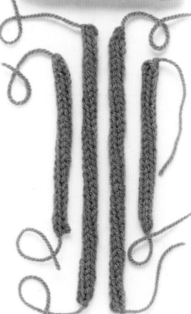

Head

Cast on 4 stitches
Row 1: Knit 4 st
Row 2: Knit 1 make 1 = 8 st
Row 3: Purl 1 make 1 = 16 st
Row 4: Knit 1 make 1 = 32 st
Row 5–18: continue in stockinette stitch, starting with a knit row.
Row 19: Knit 2 together = 16 st
Row 20: Purl 2 together = 8 st
Row 21: Knit 2 together = 4 st
Row 22: Knit 2 together = 2 st
Row 23: Knit 2 together = 1 st
Cast off.

Body and Bodice

Cast on 20 st
Stockinette stitch for 19 rows, starting with knit stitch.
Change color to body color.
Knit 3 rows in body color.
Cast off.

Arms and legs

Using a knitting spool (see page 82) and matching yarn.
Knit two 4in (10cm) cords for the arms.
Knit two 7in (18cm) cords for the legs.

Sew on beads for her earrings.

Decorate with buttons to look like jewels.

The stockinette-stitch skirt will roll up naturally.

Tie the bow at the front or the back.

New clothes
You can mix and match your doll's clothes by changing her skirts and adding more buttons and beads.

Make the head

Use the long ends to sew up the head. Make sure the seam is at the back of the head. Stuff it so it makes a good ball shape.

Turn the knitting inside out.

Using one of the long ends, sew up the sides.

Leave an opening for stuffing.

Stuff the head until it feels firm, but don't overfill it!

Use the other long end to sew up the hole.

Make the body

Knit the body shape and sew up the sides, but remember to move the seam to the center of the back. Don't overstuff.

Fold the knitting over. Sew the edges together.

Move the seam to the center and sew up the top.

Turn the body the right way out and stuff.

Sew up the opening.

Make the arms and legs

Thread the knitting spool and make the braid the required length. Tuck away one of the ends and leave the other one.

Leave long ends to the braids.

Finish off one end of the braid and leave the other end long.

Trim yarn.

Put the body together

Once all the body parts are made, they are ready to be attached. Sew in place until they are firmly attached.

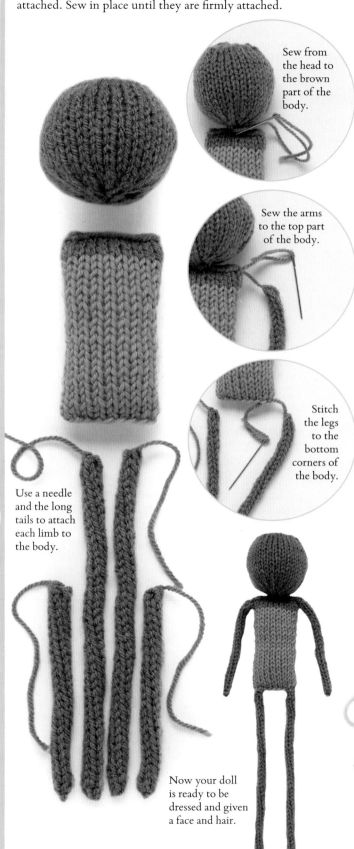

Sew from the head to the brown part of the body.

Sew the arms to the top part of the body.

Stitch the legs to the bottom corners of the body.

Use a needle and the long tails to attach each limb to the body.

Now your doll is ready to be dressed and given a face and hair.

Make the hair

Decide how long the hair should be. Once it is sewn in place it can be styled by cutting it shorter and making bangs.

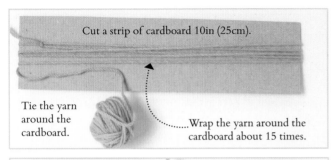

Tie the yarn around the cardboard.

Cut a strip of cardboard 10in (25cm).

Wrap the yarn around the cardboard about 15 times.

Slide the yarn off.

Tie the middle with a short length of yarn.

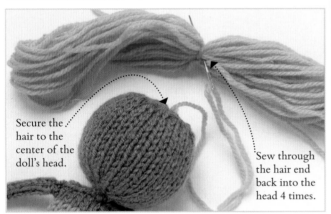

Secure the hair to the center of the doll's head.

Sew through the hair end back into the head 4 times.

Make the face

Knot the end of a short length of yarn, and push the needle into the side of the head, bringing it out where the eye will be. Make two stitches, then push the needle back out beside the knot.

Cut off the knot and the rest of the yarn.

Repeat these steps for the other eye and the mouth.

Make a skirt

This skirt is gathered at the top to fit the doll's waist, and stitched at the back. The "V" pattern is made by knitting in pink and red yarn.

Skirt Cast on 40 st
Knit the first row and continue in stockinette stitch until the knitting measures 3in (7cm). Cast off.

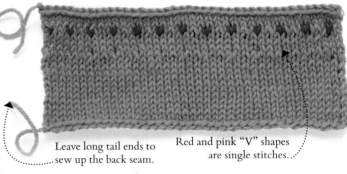

Leave long tail ends to sew up the back seam.

Red and pink "V" shapes are single stitches.

To make the pink and red "V" shapes, join the red yarn to the blue yarn at the beginning of a row. Start knitting with the blue yarn, then every fourth stitch use the red yarn instead. At the end of the row, knot the two colors together and cut off the red yarn.

The red yarn is carried along the row with the blue yarn.

Fold the knitting in half.

Stitch the two sides together.

Sew yarn around the top of the skirt.

Start at the center front.

Tie the ends into a bow.

Pull the ends of the yarn to gather the skirt.

Stockinette stitch will roll up at the edges.

Pom-poms

Pretty pom-poms are fun to make and are a decorative addition to lots of projects. Sew them to the end of a scarf or use to top a hat. They're a great way to use up short scraps of yarn—try making multicolored balls, too.

You will need

Two cardboard disks, 4in (10cm) across

3ft (1m) of yarn, plus 7in (18cm) extra to tie the pom-pom

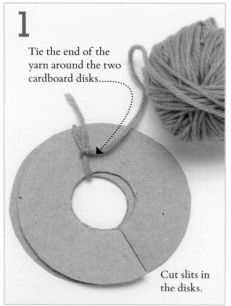

1

Tie the end of the yarn around the two cardboard disks.......

Cut slits in the disks.

2

Wind the yarn around and around the disks; the more yarn, the fuller the pom-pom.

3

Slip the scissors between the two disks and cut the yarn all the way around.

Hold the center of the disks firmly.

4

Place a 4in (10cm) length of yarn between the disks.

5

Pull the yarn tightly and tie into a knot.

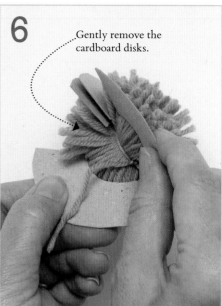

6

Gently remove the cardboard disks.

Big or small?
To make different-sized pom-poms, simply use bigger or smaller cardboard disks and follow the steps in the same way.

For a really neat shape, snip away the ends of the yarn so they are all the same length.

Use up scraps of yarn that are too short to use for knitting and wrap them around the cardboard.

Crochet

It's all about pulling loops
through loops to create a piece of fabric,
working with only one stitch at a
time—now all you need
is a hook and some yarn.

Size 7 (4.5mm)
crochet hook

L-11 (8mm)
crochet hook

Crochet hooks

Hooks are available in many
different sizes—the larger the
hook, the larger the stitch.
The projects that follow are
made using a medium-sized
7 (4.5mm) hook. Try using a
metal hook, since the yarn
moves more freely than it
does on a plastic one.

Yarn

The projects in this book are
made with cotton yarn in a
DK weight. This cotton yarn
is not fluffy like some wool
yarns. This makes it the
perfect yarn to use when
you are learning how to
crochet, because it's easy
to see the stitches.

Stitch types

When following crochet patterns, the stitch
names sometimes appear in a shortened form.
Here is a guide:

ch = chain stitch
sc = single crochet (double crochet in UK);
hdc = half double crochet (half treble crochet in
UK); dc = double crochet (treble in UK);
sl st = slip stitch

How to get started

Working loop

Crochet hook

Stitches

Rows

Unlike knitting, which uses two needles and where the working stitches are all on the needles, crochet is worked with a hook and only one stitch is made at a time.

This has been worked in single crochet

HOW TO HOLD the work

Wrap the yarn around your left hand, as shown here.

Hold the hook in your right hand.

Slip knot
The first stitch on the hook is knotted so the yarn stays on.

1 Make a loop with the end of the yarn around your fingertips.

2 Push the yarn through the loop with your index finger.

3 Pull the yarn through.

4 Transfer the loop onto the hook and pull gently on the yarn.

Foundation chain
The number of stitches on the chain will determine the width of the crochet fabric.

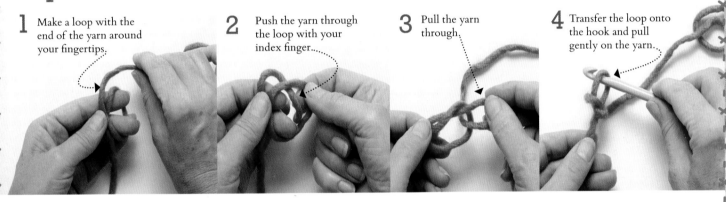

1 Hold the slip knot firmly between finger and thumb.

2 Push the hook under the yarn and catch it with the hook.

3 Pull the hook back through the stitch.

4 The stitch is complete.

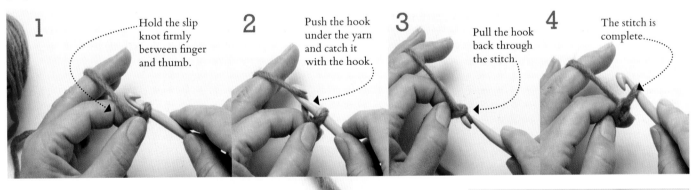

REPEAT STEPS 1–4 to continue the chain.

This foundation chain has 10 stitches—count the "V" shapes.

Make as many chain stitches as the pattern requires.

1 2 3 4 5 6 7 8 9 10

The back of the stitches will look very knobbly.

Single crochet

How to start Once you have made the foundation chain, you are ready to start crocheting. With any type of stitch you use you will need to make chain stitches at the beginning of each row so that your work is brought up to the right height.

First row in single crochet

Single crochet This basic stitch is useful for all kinds of projects. It produces a close, firm fabric.

Chain stitch At the beginning of the single stitch row, make one chain stitch. This way, when you begin to work across the row you will begin at the right height.

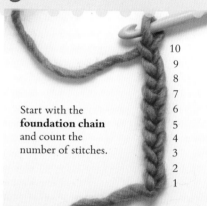

Start with the **foundation chain** and count the number of stitches.

10
9
8
7
6
5
4
3
2
1

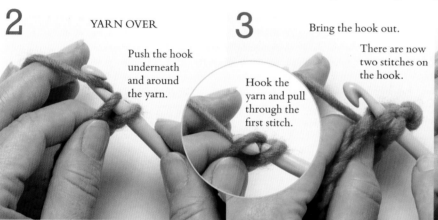

2 YARN OVER

Push the hook underneath and around the yarn.

3 Bring the hook out.

There are now two stitches on the hook.

Hook the yarn and pull through the first stitch.

4 Push the hook underneath and around the yarn. YARN OVER

Hook the yarn and pull through both stitches.

Second row in single crochet

(Use this method for all the single crochet rows from now onward.)

1 Begin the row with a **chain stitch** so there are 11 stitches.

11

1 2 3 4 5 6 7 8 9 10

NOTE: It's always one chain stitch for single crochet.

2 YARN OVER

Push the hook under the "V" of the second stitch (10th stitch).

Hook the yarn and pull through the stitch.

3 Bring the hook out.

There are now two stitches on the hook.

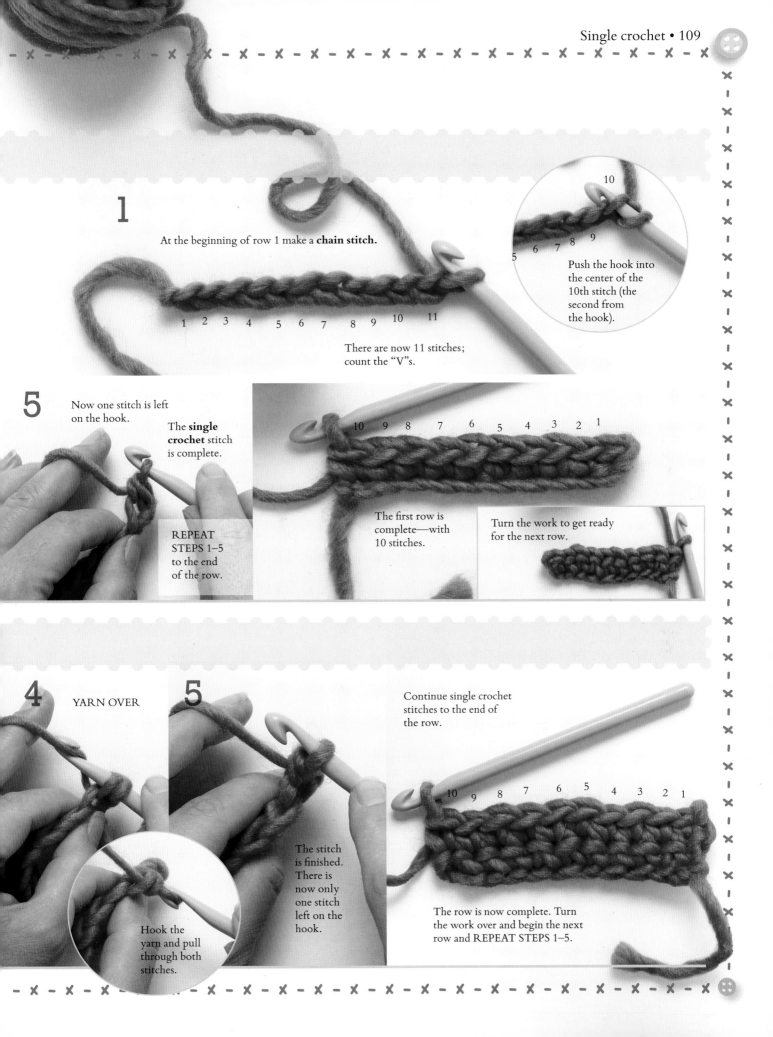

1

At the beginning of row 1 make a **chain stitch.**

1 2 3 4 5 6 7 8 9 10 11

There are now 11 stitches; count the "V"s.

Push the hook into the center of the 10th stitch (the second from the hook).

10 9 8 7 6 5

5

Now one stitch is left on the hook.

The **single crochet** stitch is complete.

REPEAT STEPS 1–5 to the end of the row.

10 9 8 7 6 5 4 3 2 1

The first row is complete—with 10 stitches.

Turn the work to get ready for the next row.

4 YARN OVER

5

The stitch is finished. There is now only one stitch left on the hook.

Hook the yarn and pull through both stitches.

Continue single crochet stitches to the end of the row.

10 9 8 7 6 5 4 3 2 1

The row is now complete. Turn the work over and begin the next row and REPEAT STEPS 1–5.

Crowls

These crocheted owls or "Crowls" are made from a strip of crochet. They make cute little soft toys and even a useful addition to your sewing kit.

You will need

- Cotton yarn for eyes and body
- Size 7 (4.5mm) crochet hook
- Soft-toy stuffing • Tapestry needle • Sewing needle and thread

How to make owls

Small owl body

Foundation chain: 10 stitches
First row: make 1 chain stitch, single crochet 10 stitches. Continue in single crochet until work measures 7in (18cm) and fasten off.

Owl eyes

Foundation chain: 2 stitches. Single crochet 10 times into the first chain stitch. Slip stitch into the first single crochet stitch and fasten off.

1 Sew in the loose ends. Fold the strip in half. Stitch the sides together.

2 Turn the work inside out.

Stuff the toy, but don't overfill.

3 Sew running stitch around the opening to close it. Pull the thread to gather up the crochet and close the hole.

4 Sew the eye in place with a sewing needle and thread.

Handy tip

Instead of stuffing the owl, you can turn it into a handy tape-measure holder. Just place the tape measure inside and lightly stitch up the opening, checking that the tape measure can run freely in and out.

Small owl

Tape measure

Place tape measure into the opening.

Sew up the opening using overstitch.

Large owl

Foundation chain: 16 stitches.

First row: Make 1 chain stitch, single crochet 16 stitches.

Continue in single crochet until work measures 10in (26cm) and fasten off.

More stitches

The following two stitches produce a different effect from single crochet. They are taller, which gives them a looser look, and they help to give the daisy petals their shape.

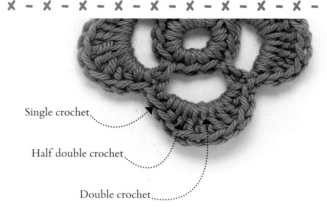

Single crochet

Half double crochet

Double crochet

Half double crochet

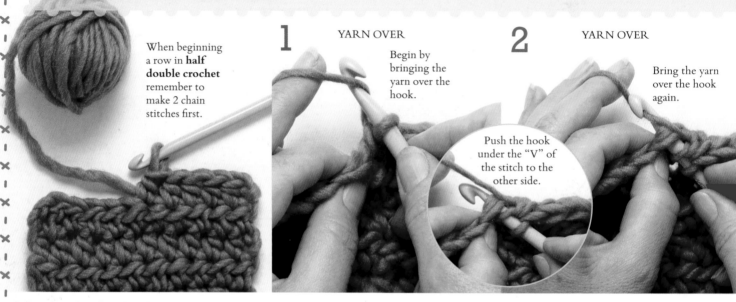

When beginning a row in **half double crochet** remember to make 2 chain stitches first.

1 YARN OVER

Begin by bringing the yarn over the hook.

Push the hook under the "V" of the stitch to the other side.

2 YARN OVER

Bring the yarn over the hook again.

Double crochet

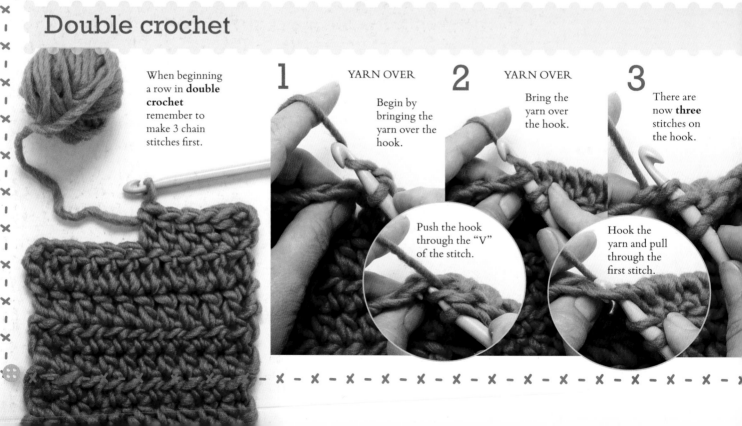

When beginning a row in **double crochet** remember to make 3 chain stitches first.

1 YARN OVER

Begin by bringing the yarn over the hook.

Push the hook through the "V" of the stitch.

2 YARN OVER

Bring the yarn over the hook.

3 There are now **three** stitches on the hook.

Hook the yarn and pull through the first stitch.

Turning chains Half double crochet and double crochet stitches require a chain stitch at the beginning of a new row, just as single crochet does:

Single crochet = 1 chain stitch
Half double crochet = 2 chain stitches
Double crochet = 3 chain stitches

These stitches are needed to bring the end of your work up to the same height as the stitch you are using.

Fasten off

When the last stitch is finished, cut the yarn and place the end in the loop.

Pull the end of the yarn to close the loop.

3
There are now three loops on the hook.

Again, hook the yarn and pull through the stitch.

4 YARN OVER
Bring the yarn over the hook.

5
Now one stitch is left on the hook.

Hook the yarn and pull through all three loops.

This completes the half double stitch.

REPEAT STEPS 1–5 to the end of the row.

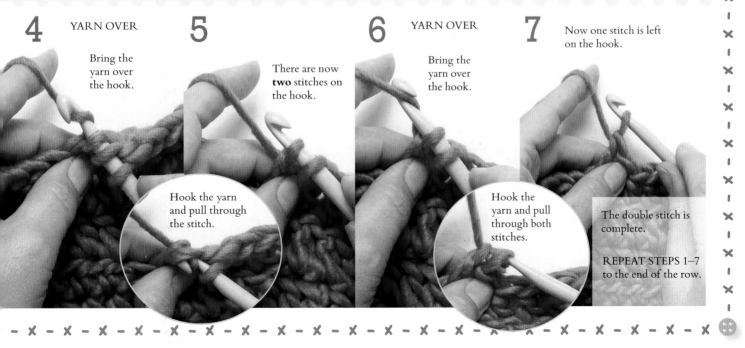

4 YARN OVER
Bring the yarn over the hook.

5
There are now **two** stitches on the hook.

Hook the yarn and pull through the stitch.

6 YARN OVER
Bring the yarn over the hook.

7
Now one stitch is left on the hook.

Hook the yarn and pull through both stitches.

The double stitch is complete.

REPEAT STEPS 1–7 to the end of the row.

4, 5, or 6 petals Once you have gotten the hang of making a four-petaled daisy, mix it up and add more petals by adapting the pattern. Each daisy is made in three stages and each also makes a pretty motif by itself.

A bunch of daisies

These fancy flowers are a perfect way to decorate your clothes and accessories. Create all kinds of variations from the number of petals to the combination of colors.

Flower brooches can be made by sewing the flowers together and finishing them with a button.

Hang a daisy from your bag. Simply loop a ribbon around a petal and tie it to the handle.

Decorate your headbands and hats with flowers, too. Here the flowers are stitched together, then sewn to the band.

Make a daisy

ch = chain stitch
st = stitch
sl st = slip stitch
sc = single crochet
hdc = half double crochet
dc = double crochet

Make a ring
Make 6 ch to join the circle; sl st to the first ch to join the ring.

Make 6 chain stitches.

Slip stitch into the first chain stitch.

The ring is complete.

Round 1
Make 1 ch, then work 12 sc into the ring, then sl st into the first ch to join together.

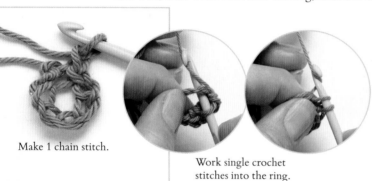

Make 1 chain stitch.

Work single crochet stitches into the ring.

Make 12 single crochet stitches.

Slip stitch into the first chain to join the round.

Round 2
Make 6 ch, ★skip 2 sc; sc into next st, 6 ch; repeat from★ to the end of the round. sl st into bottom of first 6 ch.

Make 6 chain stitches.

Skip 2 single crochet and single crochet into the next stitch.

Make 6 chain stitches.

Skip 2 single crochet and single crochet into the next stitch.

Continue to the end of the round.

Slip stitch into the first chain stitch.

Round 3
★Work (1 sc, 1 hdc, 5 dc, 1 hdc, 1 sc) into next 6 ch space; sl st into sc; repeat from ★ to the end of the round.

To make the petal shape, crochet a sequence of stitches as follows:

Work the stitches into the 6 chain space.

Continue around all four petals.

Slip stitch into the single crochet for the first petal.

6 chain space.

1 single crochet st
1 half double stitch
5 double stitches
1 half double stitch
1 single crochet st

Crochet patterns

Reading a pattern can be confusing at first, because all the words and instructions have been shortened. Use the abbreviations to the left as a handy guide to the stitch names.

The symbol ★ works like parentheses. Everything between the ★ symbols is a sequence of stitches that are repeated.

You will need
• Size 7 (4.5mm) crochet hook • yarn

3 shapes to make
Each round of the daisy makes a cute shape all on its own.

Round 1

Rounds 1 and 2

Rounds 1, 2, and 3

5 and 6 petals

To make more petals, simply add more single crochet stitches into the ring as follows.

5 petals Make a ring as before. Round 1: make **15** single crochet stitches into the ring. Round 2: work as usual.

6 petals Make a ring as before. Round 1: make **18** single crochet stitches into the ring. Round 2: work as usual.

Slip stitch (sl st)

This stitch is used to join stitches.

With 1 loop on the hook, hook into the next stitch, catch the yarn and pull the loop through the stitch and loop in one movement.

One stitch left on hook.

Make a brooch

Layer the flowers and sew them together.

Attach a button to the center.

Sew a safety pin to the back of the flower.

Stitch over and over the back of the pin to secure it.

Bags of stripes

Changing colors is a fun way to liven up a simple strip of single crochet. A length of crochet is useful for lots of projects; here, it's used to make a handy bag.

You will need

- Cotton yarn in various colors
- Size 7 (4.5 mm) crochet hook
- Tapestry needle • Button

This row is worked in double crochet.

Remember to chain 3 stitches at the start of the row.

How to change colors

Crochet to the end of the row. Turn the work as usual, then cut off the old yarn, leaving a tail about 4in (10cm) long. Loop the new color over the hook, leaving a tail about 4in (10 cm) long and pull it through the loop on the hook to make a stitch. Tug on the ends to pull the yarn tight. Continue working in the new color, with the first stitch as the chain stitch.

Neaten up the loose ends by sewing them along the edge of the work.

Thread the ends onto the tapestry needle.

BAG PATTERN

Foundation chain: 16 stitches.
Row 1: make 1 chain stitch, work 16 stitches in single crochet.
Continue working rows in single crochet, changing colors to create stripes.
In this design the stripes are 3 to 4 rows deep, but the number of stripes is up to you. This length of crochet measures 12in (30cm).

Fold the work over, leaving room at the top for the flap.

Stitch the two edges together using overstitch.

Sew up both sides and turn the work inside out.

This row is worked in double crochet.

Cut a piece of yarn 4in (10cm)

MAKE A BUTTON LOOP Push the hook through the crochet, loop the yarn over the hook, and pull the hook back through the crocheted piece. Finish the loop and sew on the button.

Place the ends through the loop and tie a knot to create a loop for the button.

Balls of yarn
Here is a collection of cotton yarn, DK weight. To make the striped bag, use up leftover lengths.

Templates

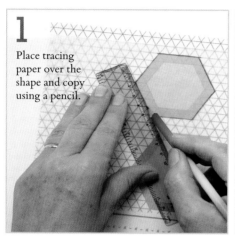

1 Place tracing paper over the shape and copy using a pencil.

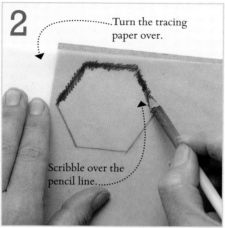

2 ....Turn the tracing paper over.

Scribble over the pencil line.....

3 ....The pencil line will transfer to the cardboard.

Transferring designs

Follow steps 1–3 to transfer the patchwork designs onto paper or cardboard.

THE BIRD AND CUPCAKE MOTIFS Because these designs aren't symmetrical, trace the shape on both sides at step one. That way, when the paper is turned over the design will be the right way around.

Large pillow
Six-sided pillow, pages 58–59

Triangle patchwork
Squares and triangles, pages 56–57

Small pin pillow
Six-sided pillow, pages 58–59

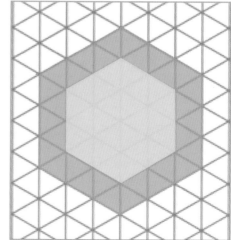

Cupcake

Cupcake motif, pages 70–71

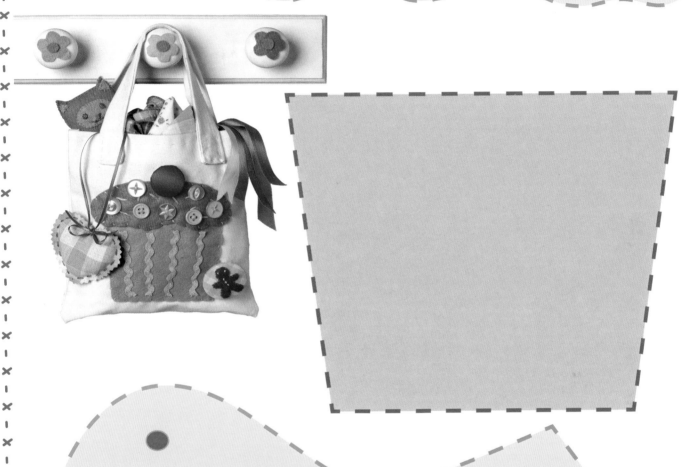

Bird

Pretty birdie, pages 26–27

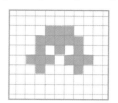

Stitching patterns

Patterns for picture stitches on pages 32–33 and pixel pictures on pages 44–45.

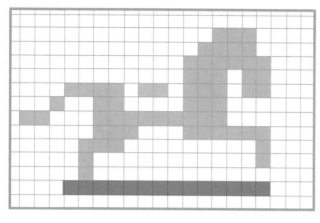

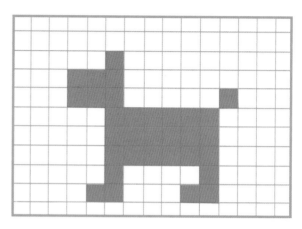

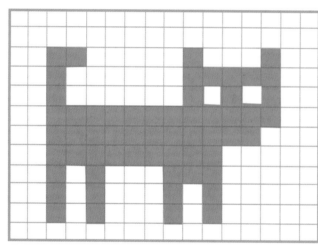

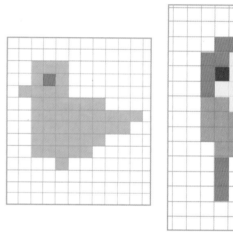

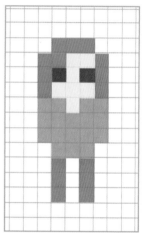

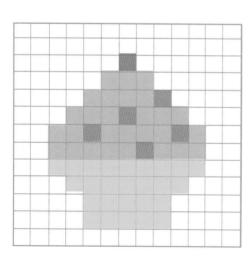

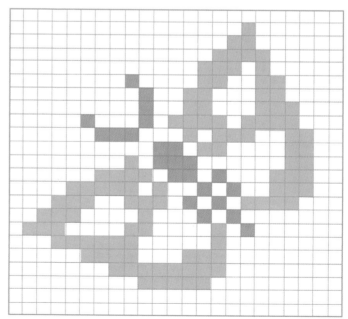

Index

Acknowledgments

Dorling Kindersley would like to thank:
Gemma Fletcher and Rosie Levine for design assistance;
David Fentiman for editorial assistance; Penny Arlon for
proofreading; Ray Williams for production help.

All images © Dorling Kindersley
For further information see: www.dkimages.com

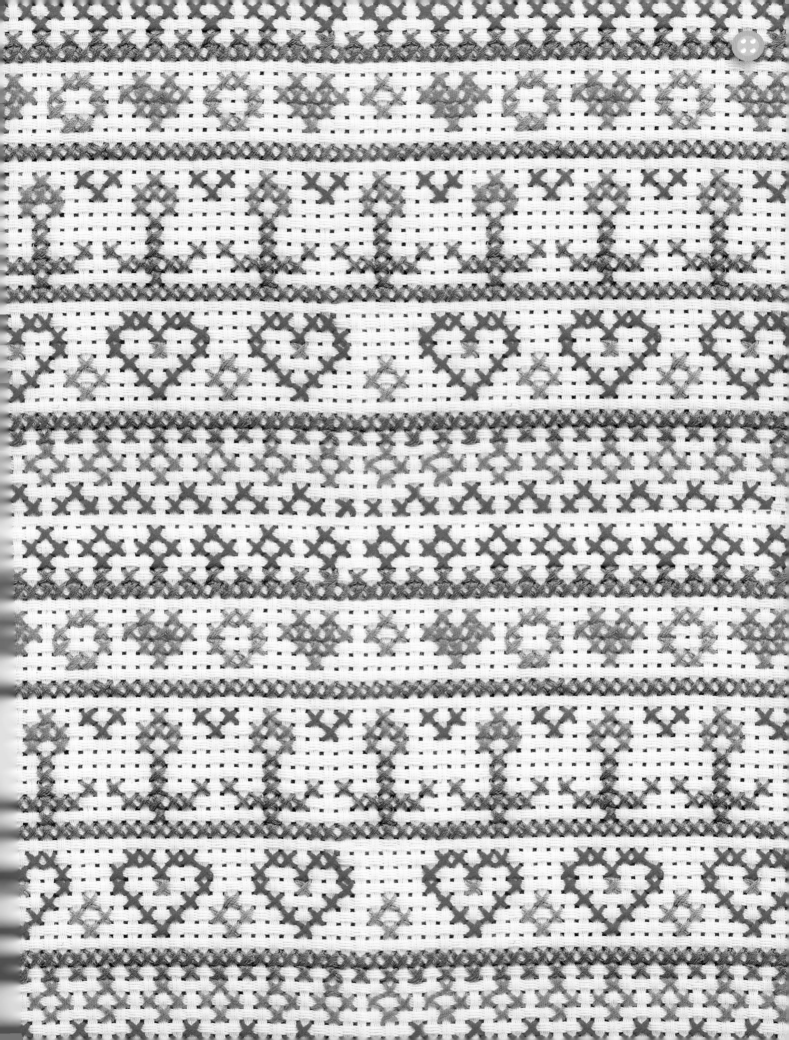